DYING
TO RELIGION
AND EMPIRE

GIVING UP OUR RELIGIOUS RITES AND LEGAL RIGHTS

JEREMY MYERS

DYING TO RELIGION AND EMPIRE:
Giving up Our Religious Rites and Legal Rights
© 2014, 2018 by Jeremy Myers

Published by Redeeming Press
Dallas, OR 97338
RedeemingPress.com

ISBN: 978-1-939992-37-6 (Paperback)
ISBN: 978-1-939992-38-3 (Mobi)
ISBN: 978-1-939992-39-0 (ePub)

LCCN: 2014957750

JOIN JEREMY MYERS AND LEARN MORE
Take Bible and theology courses by joining Jeremy at
RedeemingGod.com/join/

Receive updates about free books, discounted books,
and new books by joining Jeremy at
RedeemingGod.com/reader-group/

TAKE THE
SKELETON CHURCH
ONLINE COURSE

Join others at
RedeemingGod.com/join/
and get all my courses for free, including
"The Skeleton Church" online course:

Thanks for reading!

Books in the *Close Your Church for Good* Series

Preface: Skeleton Church
Vol. 1: The Death and Resurrection of the Church
Vol. 2: Put Service Back into the Church Service
Vol. 3: Church is More than Bodies, Bucks, & Bricks
Vol. 4: Dying to Religion and Empire
Vol. 5: Cruciform Pastoral Leadership

Books in the *Christian Questions* Series

What is Prayer?
What is Faith? (Forthcoming)
Can I Be Forgiven? (Forthcoming)
How Can I Avoid Hell? (Forthcoming)
What are Spiritual Gifts? (Forthcoming)
How Can I Study the Bible? (Forthcoming)

Other Books by Jeremy Myers

Nothing but the Blood of Jesus
The Atonement of God
The Bible Mirror (Forthcoming)
The Re-Justification of God: A Study of Rom 9:10-24
Adventures in Fishing for Men
Christmas Redemption
Why You Have Not Committed the Unforgivable Sin
The Gospel According to Scripture
The Gospel Dictionary

All books are available at Amazon.com
Learn about each title at the end of this book

*For all who were killed by religion and empire
because they died to religion and empire.*

Religion as ideology is one of the most evil and destructive forces on earth. If ever Satan created a weapon of mass destruction, his greatest success was in leading people to degrade faith into religion and religion into ideology. Binding religion to politics is to secularize the Church. It is a re-crucifixion of Christ and an utter betrayal of His Gospel.
—Vladika Lazar

TABLE OF CONTENTS

INTRODUCTION

There have been some who were so
preoccupied with spreading Christianity that they never
gave a thought to Christ.
—C. S. Lewis

One of my favorite artists is M. C. Escher. Whether or not you know who he is, you have probably seen some of his art. One famous drawing of his shows a line of sentries marching up the stairs which run along the top of a castle wall. Initially, nothing seems out of the ordinary about this drawing, but as you look closer, you discover that the stairs which circle around the castle don't have a beginning or an end. They rise infinitely. The sentries marching along the wall will never get to the top.

In another drawing, M. C. Escher drew a picture of a hand drawing a picture of a second hand which was drawing a picture of the first hand. Another famous drawing shows some flying geese morphing into swimming fish. Much of Escher's art reveals these sorts of impossibilities and illusions which look good on paper to the casual glance, but are impossible in real life.

9

Interestingly, my favorite Christian music artist, Steve Taylor, once wrote a song about the art of M. C. Escher. He named the song "Escher's World," but I think the song is actually about the world we currently live in. Part of the chorus says this:

> *Up's down, down is out, out is in.*
> *Stairways circle back to where you've been.*

Steve Taylor has properly understood the meaning of M. C. Escher's art. We live in an upside down world, but because it is familiar to us, we don't know that everything is backwards, upside down, and inside out. We think that the way things are, are the way things should be. Yet much of life is futile and empty. We endlessly strive to make sense out of life, but all we seem to do is circle back to where we've been.

The church is not immune to this problem. In fact, I firmly believe that the church is part of the problem. Like the art of M. C. Escher, much of what we believe and live for looks good on paper, but offers little value to the "real" world. As a theologian, I am always amazed at how little of my theology "works." The nicely-arranged and cleverly-alliterated three-point answer to a difficult theological question is easily obliterated by the most common of life's pains, struggles, and trials. When this happens, the question then becomes, "Is my theology wrong, or is my experience wrong?" I suspect it is a bit of both.

Without a doubt we live in an upside down world. Due to sin, our experience of life is not the way it should be. Therefore, our experience of life needs to be re-imagined. When bad things happen to us, we must not simply accept our fates, but must instead recognize that things are the way they are because they are broken. Instead of saying, "It is what it is," we can say, "It is what it has become ... but it wasn't meant to be that way, and doesn't have to stay that way." We can imagine and accomplish change.

Theology, then, lives in this strange shadow land where we can come up with neat and tidy three-point answers of "How things should be," but which don't actually apply to "How things are." This doesn't necessarily mean that the tidy answer is wrong; it simply means the tidy answer doesn't *yet* apply. Our theological answers often reflect a state of affairs in the Kingdom of God which have not yet been fully realized. One day they will be, but not yet.

In the meantime, the answers of theology must be shaped and molded by the broken experience of life. Yet at the same time, we must seek to move our experiences of life toward the reimagined state of affairs that will exist in the fully-realized Kingdom of God. To put it another way, theology must be guided by life, and life must be guided by theology. This is what many of the greatest theologians in church history meant when they spoke about testing and trying their theology in the crucible of life.

Let me provide a concrete example. Isaiah 11:6 speaks of a wolf lying with a lamb, a leopard with a young goat, and a lion with a calf. This is a picture of the peace that will exist upon the earth when Jesus rules and reigns over all. Clearly, no such peace exists today in either the animal realm or those of human governments. War and violence rage about us all the time, even in so-called "Christian" nations. Even among "Christian" churches, there is plenty of hurt, anger, resentment, gossip, slander, and betrayal.

So what are we to say about the theology of Isaiah 11:6 in light of our experience in life? The theological answer is that Jesus brings peace. The practical answer is that He doesn't. What are we to make of this seeming contradiction between the claims of theology and the experience of life? First, we must honestly admit what is really going on around us, and then we must recognize that what is going on is not what could be or should be occurring. Interpreting life theologically is not about painting a smiley-face on bad situations; it is about owning up to the reality of sin and evil around us, and then moving those situations toward redemption. This is similar to what Walter Brueggemann calls *Prophetic Imagination*.[1] We see the reality of the way things are, but then, using our knowledge of what God is like as revealed in Jesus Christ, and knowing what God intended the world to be, we imagine a way that life could be different. But we don't stop with imagination; we move toward turning that "imaginary" world into reality. We incarnate the rule and reign of God on earth.

This book is an attempt at imagination. But it is not *only* imagination. I am working to bring the things I write about in this book to reality in my own life, and I hope that what I write will encourage you to do the same.

This book looks at two of the realms in which most people live every day and in which we simply accept the way things are. It then uses theology to imagine a way that things could be different.

---

[1] Walter Brueggemann, *The Prophetic Imagination* (Minneapolis: Augsburg Fortress, 2001).

The two realms are that of religion and empire. More specifically, this book considers several of the central symbols and practices within these two realms, the religious rites we observe on a weekly and monthly basis, and the legal rights that protect how we live and function in Western society. Only when we recognize "the way things are" with our religious rites and legal rights, can we then imagine a way they could be different in light of the ever-expanding rule and reign of God on earth.

The first part of the book is about transforming the religious rites of baptism and the Lord's Supper into something that more accurately reflects the symbolism and significance of these events when they were first done by Jesus. In this section, I try to imagine how we can replace the traditional religious rites of baptism and the Lord's Supper with practices that reveal the sacrificial love and whole-hearted service that were inherent within these actions when first practiced by Jesus and the early church.

The second part of the book is about willingly sacrificing our "God-given," constitutional rights for the sake of others. It is not uncommon for people (even Christians) to sue others because their "rights" were violated. This section tries to imagine what would happen if, for the sake of the gospel, rather than sue people over our rights, we followed Paul's advice in 1 Corinthians 6:7: "Why not rather be wronged?"

Undoubtedly, many Christians will get concerned about a book that raises questions about the religious "rites" of baptism and the Lord's Supper, or our legal "rights" to things like free speech, the freedom of religion, or the right to bear arms. If this describes you, let me attempt to alleviate your fear. I am not seeking to do away with either our "rites" or our "rights;" I am seeking to redeem them in light of the death and resurrection of Jesus Christ.

Let me put it another way: If, in our efforts to protect our "rites" and our "rights" we are ruining our witness and destroying the clarity of the gospel, this is an indication that we have made idols of such things, and they need to be brought once again into subservience to Jesus Christ. The gospel of Jesus Christ is not about defending our religious rites or our legal rights, but about sacrificing everything for the sake of others. Once we die to both our rites and our rights, only then can they rise again in Jesus Christ to be used in the expansion of His rule and reign on earth. Only in this way can that which is upside down and inside out be turned right way around again.

PART I:
GIVE UP YOUR RITES

*When we seek to justify ourselves by performing the
tenets of some religious law, we can only feel guilty for
failing or self-righteous for succeeding—but never at
peace with God. When we let religion interpose between us and primary experience, we lose the very reality religion itself describes as ultimate.*
—Walter Wink

There is a world religion in which the people believe they can
please God by performing certain rites. An outside observer who
knew nothing of the teaching and tradition about these rites
might think that they were magical ceremonies. Two rites in particular are important to this religion, and in both cases, the rites
do appear to be magical in nature.

Both rites are presided over by a person who usually wears
some sort of special clothing or robes. To begin the rites, he
speaks arcane words over various elements which will be used for
these religious rites. These words are thought to instill special
spiritual qualities into the physical elements which make them

particularly effective for this rite. After the words of power have been spoken by this cleric, the practitioners of this religion who wish to participate in the rite are invited forward.

The practitioners have a part to play in these rites as well. They have usually been instructed beforehand on the special clothing they must wear, the words they must speak, and the way they must behave. They are told that if they perform their part correctly, there god will be pleased, and they will receive special power, abilities, and blessings from him. If, however, they perform their part in the rite incorrectly, not only will their god not work on their behalf, he may actually make them sick or strike them dead.

In one of these rites—which is usually a rite of initiation—the primary element used is water. While any type of water can be used, it is preferable to use fresh water from a stream or river. The cleric, who has been trained in these matters, will usually say some sort of words over the water to transform it into water with special qualities which makes it useful for this rite. After this, the initiates are invited to enter the water, where they also say certain words they have been instructed to speak. Then the initiates are washed in the water, using various methods which differ from group to group.

If the rite has been performed properly, the initiate is considered to now be blessed eternally by God, to have received special insight and power from Him, and to be part of God's chosen few. Usually, this first type of religious rite is only performed once in a person's life, though some groups perform it much more frequently.

In the second rite, which is observed much more often than

the rite of initiation by water, the cleric says words over some small items of food which are then considered to be instilled with special power from God to make a person more like Him. Usually, only those who have undergone the first rite of initiation are allowed to participate in this second rite. The practitioners are invited to eat the food that has been blessed by the cleric, but are cautioned once again that if they are unworthy to eat this food, God may strike them dead.

If this second rite is performed correctly, it too is thought to instill special characteristics and qualities in the life of those who practice it, including the forgiveness of sins, special blessings for life, and the immediate passage into eternal bliss after death.

Both of these rites have been around for thousands of years, but in recent centuries, some clerics of this religion have grown uncomfortable with the "magical" appearance of these rites, and so while they continue to practice them, they do so only in a symbolic way. They teach that these rites are not magical in any way, but are simply *reminders* about some of the central teachings within this particular religion.

Nevertheless, whether these rites are being performed by clerics who believe in the power of these rites or whether the clerics only perform them in a symbolic fashion, all agree that the rites must be observed on a regular basis. Those who wish to be part of this religion must perform these rites, for it is taught that a refusal to participate in these rites is an act of rebellion against God. If a person fails to observe one or both of these rites, such a person is not considered to be a true practitioner of the religion, and the clerics will often challenge such people to decide whether or not they really want to be part of this religion.

What is this religion? It is Christianity.

And what are the rites? Baptism and communion.[1]

THE CHRISTIAN RITES

Despite what is taught in most churches, neither baptism nor communion are necessary to be a follower of Jesus—at least, not as baptism and communion are typically practiced in the average church. I imagine that even suggesting such a thing will get me condemned as a heretic and false teacher by some, which just goes to show how critically central these rites have become in the practice of the Christian religion.

If you tell people they don't need church buildings and pastors to be the church, most will shrug their shoulders and say, "Fine. However you want to do church ..." But if you say that baptism and communion are not necessary, it is then that people start to feel threatened. These, after all, are marks of the true Christian! These are commanded by Jesus Himself! Baptism is the first step of discipleship! Communion (or the Eucharist) summarizes and encompasses everything important about Christian faith and practice! If you throw these out, you are no longer a Christian. If you do not require these, you are playing with people's eternal destinies! God will not be pleased!

I find these sentiments about baptism and communion to be true even among those Christians who do not consider themselves

---

[1] For more on the mystical and sacred evolution of these rites, see Jacques Ellul, *The Subversion of Christianity* (Grand Rapids: Eerdmans, 1986), 62-66.

to be "religious." It is common in some streams of Christianity to hear people say, "Christianity is a relationship; not a religion," yet it turns out that even among these "non-religious" Christians, baptism and communion are non-negotiable. These two ceremonies are off the table, beyond discussion, unassailable, and untouchable. To question or challenge them is to question and challenge the bedrock of Christianity.

If you don't believe me, go in next Sunday to your pastor and tell him that you have been doing some evangelism at work and several people have received eternal life. Your pastor will most likely congratulate you, and encourage you to continue your efforts. Then tell your pastor that some of these new converts asked about getting baptized, and you told them that baptism was not necessary. The response will fall somewhere between confusion and disappointment, to shock and outrage. You will also be confronted with a long list of Bible verses which command believers to get baptized. It is possible your pastor might even question your *own* salvation for having such opinions.

You could do the same thing with communion. Go into your pastor's office next week and tell him that the church should stop offering communion every month (or however often you do it). Tell him that you think communion is a waste of time and money. Then step back and see what he says. Once again (and depending on your church's view of communion), you will get a quick theology lesson about the commands to observe the Lord's Supper and how such a practice is necessary for the life and vitality of the church. You will be strongly encouraged to reconsider your views on this subject, and maybe even to reconsider whether or not you really want to be a member of that particular church.

I might be slightly overstating the reaction you would get in such scenarios, but not by much. It really does seem that in most churches, you can question and challenge almost anything, except the practices of baptism and communion. Even some of the most "progressive" of churches mandate baptism for new believers, and observe communion on a regular basis.

I once visited a church in Denver that used Coca-Cola and donuts for communion instead of grape juice (or wine) and bread, but they nevertheless taught that communion was necessary for all true believers as a sign of their communion with God and with each other, and as a reminder of what Jesus had done for us on the cross. I wasn't sure how Coke and donuts reminded us of Jesus' death, but I let it slide. Besides, I like donuts. As a side note, for a baptism ceremony, they went out and had everyone run around in the lawn while the sprinkler system was turned on. I am not making this up.

So whether we are talking about the traditional forms of baptism and communion as practiced by the majority of churches, or the more "progressive" approaches that have been adopted in others, almost all churches, of all sizes, from all denominations and traditions, practice some mode of baptism and communion. And almost all consider the "sacraments" of baptism and communion as marks of the "true" church.

But as we will see, the way these ceremonies are conducted today borders more on the magical and arcane than on the way originally practiced or commanded by Jesus. And when we understand how and why Jesus and the early church practiced baptism and communion, we will see that such practices are not required or necessary today. There are, however, helpful alternatives which seem to fit better with the original intent and purpose of baptism and communion, and which will be recommended and suggested later in this book.

THE RITE SYMBOLISM

Ultimately, there is nothing wrong with practicing baptism and communion (also referred to as "the Lord's Supper"). In the days when they were initiated and practiced, both were meaningful and helpful for the teaching of the apostles and the life of the early church. Both practices had deep and rich significance.

The genius of these ceremonies was that they taught the central beliefs and core doctrines of Christianity in forms that were commonly practiced in the culture of that day. In other words, they didn't invent these rites; the rites were already in existence in their day, and the Christians adopted these rites as their own, and instilled them with new meaning. They "redeemed" the rites.

Take baptism, for example. John the Baptist did not invent baptism, nor did Jesus or the early church. Baptism was a practice already widely used among numerous groups in that day and culture. It already had clear symbolism and significance. John the Baptist and the early church simply took a ceremony which was already in use by the culture and redirected the symbols and significance to Jesus.

The same is true of the Lord's Supper. N. T. Wright has said, "When Jesus wanted to explain to His followers what He thought would be the meaning of His death, He did not give them a theory; He gave them a meal."[2] While this is true, I would like to slightly amend what N. T. Wright has said. Jesus didn't exactly give them a meal; He gave *new meaning* to a meal the Jews already observed. The meal Jesus gave them already existed among the Jews, was observed by them annually, and was full of inherent significance and meaning. He took a meal which the Jewish people were already eating on a regular basis, which was already full of symbolism and significance, and then redirected all of the symbols and meaning to Himself. Jesus "fulfilled" the meal. Jesus added new meaning to an already meaningful meal.

We will explain the pre-Christian practice of baptism and the Lord's Supper later, but for now, it is critical to grasp *why* the Christian adopted and adapted the religious traditions that were already present in their culture.

Part of it was because this is the way people learned. They did not live in a literate society, which meant that people did not learn by reading, but by hearing, observing, and doing. Where people cannot read, truth is often passed down through traditions, customs, ceremonies, stories, and celebrations.

Another reason early Christians adopted and adapted the traditions of their culture is because this practice put on display God's work of redemption. Redemption is one of the primary works of God in this fallen world, whereby He takes people, places, customs, traditions, and cultures that were previously in bondage to sin and death, and transforms these things into instruments

---

[2] N. T. Wright, "Reading Paul, Thinking Scripture," in *Scripture's Doctrine and Theology's Bible* (Grand Rapids: Baker, 2008), 59-71.

of love and light so that the rule and reign of God expands upon the earth. Just as God redeemed a people for Himself through the nation of Israel, and then also through the church, so also, God is in the business of redeeming all things for His own purposes, including customs, traditions, and cultures.

One final reason that Jesus and the early church adopted and adapted the religious traditions and customs of Judaism was that this practiced created bridges of meaning and symbolism with the culture. Their goal was not to appear weird, strange, mystical, magical, or unearthly, but to communicate the truth of the gospel in ways that were already familiar to the surrounding culture.

When someone who was not a Christian saw a friend or neighbor eating this meal or getting baptized, they did not think the practice was strange. They did not wonder what it meant. For the most part, they already knew what these ceremonies meant, for they were commonly practiced by all people at that time. The one thing they would not have known was the particular *reason* or *purpose* for these ceremonies. And so they would have asked, which provided the Christian with an opportunity to tell someone about Jesus.

If, for example, a man saw his neighbor getting baptized in a river, they would have immediately understood the symbol and significance of this action, but would not have known *why* the person was getting baptized. So they would have asked, "Why did you get baptized?" The Christian would then have an opportunity to explain that they were now following Jesus. Using the commonly practiced ceremonies of their culture were natural ways for believers to create conversations with friends and neighbors about following Jesus.

To make this clear, the following two chapters will look at the historical meaning and Scriptural passages regarding baptism and the Lord's Supper, and what these ceremonies would have meant in the days of Jesus and the early church. Only then can we ask whether or not baptism and the Lord's Supper accomplish the same purpose today, or if we might be wiser to choose some other type of ceremony to accomplish these same purposes.

DISCUSSION QUESTIONS

1. Do you believe that baptism and communion are required for a person to become (or remain) a Christian? Why or why not?

2. Do you think the average non-Christian today understands the symbolism and significance of Christian baptism or communion? What might they think if they saw some people performing these religious ceremonies?

3. What, if anything, do you think the religious rites of baptism and communion tell the average non-Christian about God?

4. If the average non-Christian in the days of Jesus and the early church immediately understood the symbolism and significance of baptism and communion when they saw Christians engaging in these practices, but the average non-Christian today does not understand the symbolism

and significance, why do so many Christians still practice these rites today?

CHAPTER 1

THE RITE OF BAPTISM

A coworker recently told me she started going to church again, and thought she should get baptized. I asked her if she had ever been baptized before. She hadn't.

So I asked her why she wanted to get baptized.

"Well," she said, "Isn't that what God wants?"

I encouraged her for her desire to obey God and do what He wants, but I also told her that God doesn't really care too much if she gets baptized or not.

She was shocked to hear me say this, as you might be as well. We are taught, almost from day one, that baptism is an essential first step for any believer. Some churches will teach that if you are not baptized, you are not even saved. I am not sure which view this woman heard at her church, so I went on to explain to her that baptism is not for God. He already loves her and forgives her and accepts her completely. Baptism was not to please or appease God, but is a public declaration of her desire to follow Jesus. When you get baptized, it is like publicly stating, "I am a follower of Jesus!" In went on to tell her that if this is what she wants to do, and she wants to make this statement through water baptism, that would be fine.

However, I explained to her that there were numerous other

ways of making a public declaration about her choice to follow Jesus, and one of those other ways might be more meaningful for her and for those who know her. We went on to talk about what some of those other ways might be, and she told me she would think about it. She said she was not sure she was ready to make any of those other public declarations.

Isn't that interesting? She was ready and willing to get baptized, but not ready to make a public declaration among her friends and family about her desire to follow Jesus.

On another occasion, a man I worked with came and told me that he wanted to get baptized. I asked him why. He said that he had made a mess of his past and wanted to have a brand new start. "Wonderful!" I said. "But what does that have to do with baptism?" He went on to say that he had been baptized before, but it "didn't take." A friend of his had told him that he had been baptized by the wrong church, and if he got baptized the "right way," then baptism would wash away his past, give him victory over sin and temptation, and provide a brand new start on the path to following God.

"Baptism is not going to do any of that for you," I told him. "It's not magical. If you want to change your habits and turn from your past behaviors, you've got to actually make some changes in your life." We then discussed some changes he could make in his life which would be of greater help in turning from his past than getting dunked under water any number of times.

Both of these encounters made me wonder. How many people who get baptized today really understand what they are supposedly doing? How many understand what baptism really represents? And if baptism today truly represented what baptism did in the days of Jesus and the early church, how many people would really undergo baptism?

Many pastors are aware of this dilemma—that most people today do not understand what baptism represents—and so they try to educate the people who receive baptism about its meaning and significance. However, I think that even this solution misses most of the symbolism and significance of baptism.

It is true (in my theology) that baptism is a sign. But it is not only a sign for the person getting baptized, it is also a sign for everybody else. Baptism is supposed to be a sign, not just for Christians, but for all people in the life of the person getting baptized—friends, family, coworkers, and neighbors. So educating the person getting baptized about the symbolism of baptism only fixes a tiny percentage of the problem.

Yet we are not even succeeding at that! If most people in the pews do not know what baptism represents, how can we possibly hope to educate the rest of the watching world? It's impossible.

However, the primary problem with baptism is not even that the vast majority of people in this world do not understand the symbolism. The real problem is that Christians often substitute baptism for what baptism is actually supposed to represent. Baptism is supposed to symbolize a changed life, a life committed and devoted to following Jesus. Yet far too often, people who are baptized exhibit no real or lasting change in their life. They undergo the rite of baptism, but they don't make any of the changes in their life. They substitute the rite for the reality.

It is a bit like the "rite" of foot washing. Have you ever been in a church that has a "Foot Washing Ceremony"? These ceremonies have to be one of the most awkward, strange, and meaningless things the church can do. At the Last Supper Jesus shared with His disciples, He set out to show them His love by taking on the appearance of a servant and washing the feet of His disciples (John 13:1-17). In John 13:15, Jesus says that His followers should do as He has done to them.

Many churches take this statement of Jesus literally by having foot washing ceremonies. People are invited to come to the front of the church, take their shoes off, and have others come wash their feet. More often than not, it is the church leadership who does the foot washing. They understand that Jesus was trying to show that leaders must serve. Usually, of course, the foot washing ceremony is announced ahead of time, and all those who want to get their feet washed make sure they wash their own feet at home before coming to the church service.

But all of this is beside the point. What most people ignore is that in first century Israel, there were people in most households who performed this foot washing service daily, if not multiple times per day. They were the lowest of the low household servants. People wore sandals all the time and while they walked around the dusty, muddy streets, which were littered here and there with cow manure and horse dung, their feet became quite disgusting. When people got home, they took their sandals off at the door and a house slave would wash the grime and filth off of people's feet before they entered the house.

Most pastors recognize and understand the cultural reasons for the foot washing of Jesus' day, but utterly fail to make a modern parallel to it. They feel that if they simply wash other people's feet, they are following the example of Jesus. Nothing could be further from the truth.

Truly following the example of Jesus does not consist of washing people's feet. This is what Jesus did, yes, but He did it because this is what was done in that culture, and people naturally and automatically understood the nature of the symbolism. Jesus showed His love by taking the form of the lowest of the low servant, and doing for His disciples what nobody else wanted to do.

If we were really going to follow the example of Jesus today, those leaders who sought to serve their people would not have a "Foot Washing Ceremony" but would instead go change diapers in a nursing home, mow a lawn for a single mother, paint the house of the widow down the street, or fix the fence for the overworked rancher.

Do you see? Following the example of Jesus is not woodenly doing whatever it is He did, but rather by understanding the culture He was in and the symbolic nature of His actions in that culture, and then seeking to find parallel actions in our own day.

This is what needs to be done with baptism. It is time to give water baptism a long-needed burial. Since it is neither wise nor possible to educate an entire generation of Christians on what baptism indicates, and also educate an entire culture of people about what it means when their friends and family members get baptized, letting baptism die would do everybody a service. Even if we could educate an entire generation and culture about the symbolism of baptism, this still would not be helpful, for then baptism only becomes a foreign rite with foreign symbolism.

So maybe it is best to let baptism die. But if we do, this does not mean that we abandon the meaning and significance that is behind baptism. No, once we let baptism die, it is then that we are able to resurrect it. Baptism can rise again from the grave.

With some creative thinking, baptism can undergo death and resurrection. It can reveal the same significance and meaning it did 2000 years ago. Best of all, this can be done without having to educate the entire world on what baptism represents.

To do this, we simply have to follow the same steps briefly revealed above in the discussion on foot washing. For the symbolism of baptism to work properly in our time and culture, the symbolism of baptism has to be understood not only by those getting baptized, but also by those who observe the baptism, including the surrounding non-Christian culture of friends, neighbors, and coworkers who hear about it. But since we cannot educate the entire world about baptism, it would be more natural, incarnational, and meaningful to find an event or ceremony *in our own culture* which symbolized the same thing that baptism symbolized in the days of Jesus and the early church, and then *use that event*, rather than water baptism, to symbolize the change that has occurred in our life.

Let us begin this process by looking back to biblical culture to relearn the meaning and significance of baptism and what it meant in that day. Only then can we begin to look for some equivalent function and symbol in our own time and culture.

BAPTISM IN BIBLE TIMES

The history of baptism does not actually begin with the New Testament and the baptism of John, but many thousands of years earlier. Baptism is not a uniquely Christian rite. Early Mesopotamian, Babylonian, Egyptian, Persian, and Eastern religions practiced various forms of baptism. A form of baptism is also a central religious rite in Hinduism, various Indigenous American religions, and of course, in Judaism. Various types of washings and purifications by water are practiced in nearly every religion in the world, including Islam, Buddhism, and Shintoism. In nearly every case, the washing with water represents purification and a movement toward holiness so that the individual worshipper may approach God to offer sacrifices or pray.[1]

Of great interest to some historians is the fact that ancient Sumerians worshipped the water god Ea at their temple in the city of Eridu. Astrological religions equate this deity with Capricorn, which is the sign of the Zodiac that indicates winter solstice, the death of the previous year and the rebirth of the new year. Of even more interest is that in Greek Hellenistic religion, the god Ea was called Oannes, or Ioannes. In English, we would say "John." As a result of this, some have taught that the accounts in the Gospels about John the Baptist were fabricated or "borrowed" from the ancient Sumerian myths. John does, after all, preach that the old way is dead, that the promised Messiah is coming who will usher in a new era of peace for the entire world, and that those who want to participate in this new era must show it by going through the waters of baptism. All of this is quite similar to what the followers of Ea would have done 3000 years earlier.[2]

It is best, however, to realize that John the Baptist was a real

[1] Albrecht Oepke, "*baptō, baptizō*" in Gerhard Kittel, ed. *Theological Dictionary of the New Testament*, 10 vols. (Grand Rapids: Eerdmans, 1964-76), I:531.

[2] Charles Panati, *Sacred Origins of Profound Things* (New York: Arcana, 1996), 167.

historical figure, and he really did come to the region of the Jordan preaching a baptism of repentance for the remission of sins, and many people came from Jerusalem and Judea to listen to him preach and to be baptized by him in the Jordan River. Jesus Himself came to be baptized by John in the Jordan (cf. Luke 3:1-22). The fact that John is preaching a baptism of repentance for the remission of sins does not seem to fit with the fact that Jesus, who was sinless, would need to get baptized by John (Matt 3:14-15). But this dilemma fades away once we begin to understand the cultural and theological significance of water baptism.

To understand this significance, let us begin by looking at the word *baptism*.

What is baptism? The wide variety of opinions on this question is revealed by the diversity of forms, methods, and teachings about baptism. Some groups baptize infants, while others baptize only adults. Some groups get baptized every year, while others will get baptized numerous times per week. There is even a group out there that gets baptized for dead people. It is no wonder that people are confused about what baptism is. Like the word "church," many of the problems surrounding baptism can be done away with simply by properly defining the word itself.[3]

The first thing we must realize about the word baptism is that, like many confusing words in Christianity, "baptism" is not a translation of a Greek word, but a transliteration. The Greek words are *baptizma* (noun) or *baptizō* (verb). You can see how

---

[3] On the definition of "church" see Jeremy Myers, *Skeleton Church: The Bare Bones Definition of Church* (Dallas, OR: Redeeming Press, 2012).

close these words are to "baptism," showing that baptism is not a translation of the Greek, but a transliteration.

Since there is so much division and strife over what the word means, Bible translators have traditionally chosen to leave the word untranslated, and just change the Greek letters of the word into English, thereby leaving it up to the individual reader to decide how to understand the word.

But what does the word actually mean? The most basic definition of the verb *baptizō* is "to dip" or "to immerse." But do not think that this solves the ancient religious debate about baptism by immersion versus sprinkling. It doesn't. While baptism means immersion, it does not imply immersion into water.

In Greek literature, "baptism" rarely refers to what we think of as "baptism with water." Instead, the word refers to a wide variety of events or ideas. It is used to refer to a sinking ship or a drowning person, and also to someone who is overcome by sickness and disease and "sinks" into death. In some Greek references, it refers to people who sink into sleep, intoxication, or impotence, or even to those who are overwhelmed by faults, desires, and the magical arts.[4]

So "baptism" does not inherently include any idea of getting dunked under water, but rather refers to being immersed, overwhelmed, or overcome by something else. When a person undergoes *baptizma,* it means they are no longer who they were before, but are now fully identified with someone or something else entirely.

[4] Oepke in Kittel, ed. *TDNT*, I:530.

Therefore, whenever you see the word "baptize" or "baptism" in Scripture, it would be wise to stop and change the word into "immersion" or "identification" and then ask yourself, "Immersed or identified with what?" This will help clear up numerous confusing passages in Scripture which talk about "baptism."

Take 1 Corinthians 10:2, for example, where Paul writes about the Israelites being "baptized into Moses in the cloud and in the sea." What does this mean? If we think of baptism only as getting dunked under water, Paul's statement is difficult to understand. But when we understand the word *baptism* to mean an immersion or a complete identification with something else, the statement becomes clearer. God protected the people of Israel by use of the pillar of cloud and fire, and God helped them escape the Egyptian army through the sea. But both of these protective actions were mediated by Moses. Divine protection was sent from God in response to the prayer of Moses on behalf of the people (Exod 14:10-31).

As a result, the people came to believe in God *and in Moses* (Exod 14:31). They saw that Moses was God's servant, and that their survival depended upon Moses interceding with God for them. Every time there was a problem, they went to Moses asking him to intercede for them. Every time they sinned and God threatened to destroy the Israelites, Moses begged for God to forgive them. From the events at the Red Sea, the people of Israel fully identified themselves with Moses, and he with them. In the cloud and in the sea, Moses and Israel became one.

With this in mind, something along the following lines would probably make a better translation of 1 Corinthians 10:2: "Israel fully identified itself with Moses in the cloud and in the sea." In support of this idea, Paul goes on to write about how they all act-ed as "one" after this, eating the same food and drinking the same drink. He goes on, however, to warn that this "unity" only went so far, and uses this point to address some of the issues that the Corinthian Christians were facing. The point for us here is that the "baptism into Moses" has nothing to do with what we nor-mally think of as baptism.

There are other examples from the New Testament we could turn to as well. Jesus refers to a baptism of the cup of suffering in Matthew 20:22 and Luke 12:50. This baptism has nothing to do with water, but instead uses the word *baptism* with its basic mean-ing of complete immersion in or full identification with some-thing else. The baptism into the cup of suffering means that Jesus would fully experience and immerse Himself into the sin, pain, and suffering of the world.

Similarly, there is the baptism of the Holy Spirit and of fire in Matthew 3:11 and Luke 3:16. Depending on how you read these passages, John could be speaking of one baptism or two: a bap-tism of the Holy Spirit upon believers and a baptism of fiery judgment upon unbelievers (cf. Matt 13:25-30, or one baptism of the Holy Spirit which will come with fire upon believers (cf. Acts 2:3). But whether John is referring to one baptism or two, noth-ing he says has anything to do with water. He is writing about being overcome or overwhelmed by whatever people are baptized into.

All of this points to the fact that even in Scripture, the word "baptism" means that the person or group getting "baptized" loses their former identity and is now fully identified with something or someone else. Israel identifies itself not as Egyptian slaves or individual people, but as a nation under the headship of Moses. On the cross, Jesus leaves the realm of joy, peace, and holiness, and fully enters the realm of pain and suffering, sin and sorrow, death and destruction. In the baptism of the Spirit, the former body of sin passes away and a new creation is born to everlasting life.

What does this mean then for the water baptisms, and not just in Christianity, but also in Judaism, and in the numerous other religions around the world and throughout time that practiced some form of baptism in water? Now that we know the definition and meaning of the word "baptism" we are able to better understand the religious significance of water baptism in these other religions, and in Christianity itself.

For most religions, water baptism was a form of ritual washing and purification before a particular ceremony, sacrifice, or religious service. It was viewed as a way to cleanse oneself both physically and spiritually before meeting with that religion's deity. In some religious circles, baptism was used as a rite of healing and exorcism. It was thought that if the water was blessed in a particular way by a priest, it had healing powers which could wash away the sickness or evil spirit. It was also customary in some regions to "baptize" or wash those who had died, so that any residual uncleanness could be removed from the body, and the spirit of the person could break free of the dead body and be released into the realm of the gods or into the renewal of life and reincarnation.

Interestingly, the Egyptians believed that it was the god Osiris himself who chose whom to baptize, and he chose them by drowning or "immersing" them in the Nile River. If a person fell

into the river and drowned, or was pulled into the river by a croc-
odile, it was believed that Osiris had specifically chosen that person for some special role in the afterlife, and the person's body
was treated as a most holy and sacred relic.

> No one may touch him, whether relatives or friends, apart from the
> priests of the Nile, who must tend him with their own hands and
> treat him as one who is more than an ordinary being. … To be
> drowned in the river is to enter into connection with the god and
> thus to be divinized.[5]

This idea fits perfectly with the idea that "baptism" or "immersion" causes the person to become completely identified with
what they were baptized into. The person who drowns or is immersed in the river, becomes identified and connected with the
river, and thus also with Osiris, the god of the river.

This sort of thinking was prevalent in nearly all forms of religion up to the times of Jesus and the apostles. This includes the
practice of baptism within Judaism. Most Christians today do not
realize that the practice of baptism was a common occurrence
within Judaism during the days of John the Baptist, Jesus, Peter,
and the apostles. In fact, since they were all Jewish, it is quite likely that the baptisms they all experienced as followers of Jesus were
not some of the first "Christian" baptisms, but were traditional
Jewish baptisms. This is especially true since all of Jesus' early
followers who underwent baptism did so before Jesus ever died
and rose from the dead. So their "baptism" could not have been a

[5] Ibid., I:433-534.

Christian baptism symbolizing our death, burial, and resurrection in Jesus Christ. Furthermore, it is important to remember that they were not trying to start a new "religion" but were simply trying to announce God's acceptance of all people into His Kingdom and plan for the world. So their baptisms would have been thoroughly Jewish.

What then is a Jewish baptism? As with other religions, there are various forms of washings and immersions in water within Judaism. The priests often washed themselves in various ways before sacrifices and ceremonies in the Temple, and men and women also had to undergo various ritual washings for other purposes.

One common form of baptism was for proselytes to Judaism. When a Gentile wanted to convert to Judaism, one of the rites of initiation was to undergo a ritual washing of purification called a *Mikvah*.

The Jewish Talmud, in the *Mikva'ot* tractate, states that when a Gentile wishes to become a Jew, he must be instructed according to the 613 commandments of the Torah, must be circumcised, and must go through a Mikvah, that is, he must be baptized. The Talmud teaches that when the convert goes under the water, he goes under as a Gentile, but when he comes back up, it is as a Jew. When he emerges from the water, he is born again like a new-born babe, with a new soul, spiritually and ritually pure.[6] It is said that just like a baby is surrounded by water in the womb, so also in a Mikvah the person is surrounded by water. And just

---

[6] Ibid., I:536.

as the baby, when it comes out of the water, is born to a new life, so also, the person who comes up out of the waters of the Mikvah is born to a new life as a Jew.

However, once a person becomes a Jew, they will often continue this practice of ritual washings throughout their life. Devout Jews will often go through numerous Mikvahs per year, sometimes as frequently as once per day. These washings are intended to purify the person from ritual impurity that occurs throughout life (cf. 2 Kings 5:24; Sirach 34:25; Mark 7:4). Undergoing the Jewish baptism is therefore a way of maintaining ritual and moral purity.

All of this indicates that the baptism of John was not a "Christian" baptism, but a Jewish baptism. The Jewish religious system and political scene had become corrupt, full of power-hungry priests and religious leaders who stole from the poor and the widows to make themselves rich so they could bribe political officials for special privileges and positions. The baptism of John was not for the purpose of calling people away from Judaism and into Christianity. Christianity didn't even exist yet. No, the baptism of John was a call to Jews to return to true and proper Judaism. Those who underwent John's baptism were expected to be generous with their money, honest in their business dealings, and gracious in their use of power over others (Luke 3:10-14). Through his preaching and call to baptism, John was simply inviting the people back to the standards and ideals which God had wanted for His people all along.

Throughout Israelite history there had always been a remnant that did not go the way of rebellion against God, but lived according to His Word and His will. Through baptism, John was calling such a remnant to make a public declaration of their desire to follow God in righteousness and faithfulness. Those who came to be baptized by John publicly declared in front of the entire crowd that when they entered the water they were part of the corrupt Judaism, but when they came back up out of the water they no longer identified with the corrupt way of doing things, but were now part of the new order of God which would follow and obey Him in righteousness and justice.

It is because of John's message of baptism and separation from the corruption of Judaism that many scholars believe that John may have been part of a Jewish sect called the Essenes. The Essenes lived in the Judean desert wilderness, and they too believed that Judaism had become corrupt. To separate themselves from the corruption, they moved out into the wilderness to live, work, and worship in a holy community. The writings of the Essenes sound similar to some of the things preached by John the Baptist, and their writings also contain instructions for the baptisms of people who join them. Archeologists have uncovered large baptismal pools where the Essenes would have undergone these ritual baptisms of separation.

But whether John was an Essene or not, the point is that in the days of John, Jesus, Peter, Paul, and the early church, the average person knew what baptism meant. Not only did every religion in the area practice some form of baptism for various reasons and purposes, but within Judaism, baptisms were a central practice. For Jews, baptism indicated a death to the past and a rising to a new life. Following the definition of baptism as "identification" or "immersion," a water baptism indicated that a person would fully identify and immerse themselves in a new way of living for the future.

All of this helps us understand why Jesus got baptized by John. When Jesus came to be baptized by John in the Jordan, He was making a public declaration about which type of Judaism He thought was best. The baptism of Jesus was not so He could get forgiveness of sins, for Jesus had not sinned. Nor was the baptism of Jesus for conversion, or to be saved, or to receive eternal life, or any such thing. No, through baptism, Jesus was rejecting the corruption that had entered the religious and political spheres of Judaism, and was choosing to side with those who sought generosity, honesty, peace, and grace.

The baptism of Jesus by John in the Jordan had nothing to do with repenting of sin or getting saved, but everything to do with making a public declaration about which side Jesus was on and what He would live for in His life. John called the people to turn away from corrupt Judaism and be restored to a new life of faithful obedience to God. Jesus responded to that call by getting baptized by John in the Jordan River. Jesus wanted to be fully immersed and identified in the values of the Kingdom of God that John was preaching.

So in Judaism, baptism in water represents a death to the past and a new birth to a completely different future. It symbolizes death, burial, and new birth. The coming up out of the water did not symbolize resurrection (for many Jewish people did not believe in the resurrection), but of being reborn out of water, like a newborn babe. This partly explains why Jesus is incredulous that Nicodemus does not understand about being "born again" (John 3:10). As a leader of Israel who had certainly undergone many ritual washings himself, and had likely performed many for others, Nicodemus should have known the "born again" symbolism of baptism. Baptism as a means of being "born again by water" was a common practice among Judaism. Entering the water was a way of identifying oneself with the purity of a newborn infant, and indicated that a person was turning away from something in their previous life and making a fresh start in a new direction.

Most everyone within Judaism understood this symbolism. So when someone was baptized, and other people observed or heard about it, they would naturally ask the person what had changed in their life. If you were a Jewish person and you heard that you neighbor got baptized, you would want to know what they were "dying" to. You would also begin to watch what their "born again" life looked like. You would see if the change they professed really did take place, or if they slipped back into their previous habits and old ways.

A lot of this should sound very similar to the instruction you received from your pastor or your church about the symbolism of baptism. This is no surprise, since Christian baptism was derived from Jewish baptism.

Of course, Christian baptism went through its own stages of evolution. Though all early Christian baptisms were done by immersion, the question was soon raised in some churches about what could be done for new converts in areas where there was very little water, or at times where there was mass conversion but very little time to baptize them all, or even in the instance where the sick or elderly could not get into a pool of water. The suggestion was raised by various church leaders that the effectiveness of baptism was not in getting dunked under water, but with the water itself. In other words, the importance of baptism was not in how much water was used, but simply *that* water was used.

Therefore, it was argued, the amount of water was not what was important, nor was it important for the new convert to be submerged beneath the water. The church decided that since it was the water which gave baptism its effectiveness rather than the immersion under water, a small portion of water could be poured or sprinkled upon the new convert. This, of course, led to the common practice in the church of baptism by sprinkling, especially for infants.

Along with these questions of how much water was to be used, some early Christians wondered how baptism could be effective if only dirty and muddy water was available. Some believed that if baptism was to purify the person, pure water was required. But in most places, clean water was not available. So the church declared that even muddy water could be used if the priest blessed it. Through such a blessing, the water now became "Holy Water" and was therefore effective for baptism, even if it remained muddy. One can see how, in an effort to minister to the people within their situation, mystical and magical elements began to be introduced into the rite of baptism. Once the ritual of baptism was boiled down to the spiritual power within the ritual, the symbolic nature of the ritual disappeared, and the emphasis fell upon the ritual itself, whether done in large quantities or little.

Was the church wrong to adapt baptism to fit the needs of the people? Some say yes; some say no. Initially, it was probably a move in the right direction by the early church, for they seemed to have understood that the significance of baptism was in the symbolism of it, rather than in the action itself. Nevertheless, over time, the mystical nature of baptism came to be emphasized, even in the act of sprinkling, until the symbolism itself vanished, and the church was left with a mystical and magical rite that was effective in imparting grace and regenerating those who got baptized. This way of thinking about baptism is common in many churches, even among those who practice baptism by immersion.

So what should be done about baptism? How should it be practiced? What, if anything, does it do for the person who undergoes baptism? To help answer these questions, it might be best to turn to some key Scriptures on baptism to better understand the symbolism that was inherent within the original baptism ceremonies of the early church.

SCRIPTURES ON BAPTISM

As we turn to look at some individual texts on baptism, we must remember everything we have learned so far. Just because a Scripture talks about "baptism," does not mean that it has water baptism in view. Remember, the definition of "baptism" is "being immersed into, overwhelmed by, or fully identified with" something or someone else. So in looking at the Scripture passages on baptism, we will first try to determine in context what kind of immersion or re-identification is in view. If the context is unclear in this regard, we will assume that since Judaism gave birth to Christianity, the baptism in question is a Jewish-style baptism, complete with being dipped, or immersed, in water, and in which a person makes a public profession of a radical change in their life by symbolically dying to the past and being born again into a new, fresh, and different future.

We will be looking at these passages: Matthew 28:19-20,

THE RITE OF BAPTISM 47

Mark 16:16, several Scriptures on baptism from the book of Acts, and Romans 6. There are other passages which speak of baptism, but these are some of the primary texts for our purposes here.

Matthew 28:19-20

Go therefore and make disciples of all the nations, baptizing them in the name of the Father and of the Son and of the Holy Spirit, teaching them to observe all things that I have commanded you; and lo, I am with you always, even to the end of the age.

When the church teaches about baptism, one of the things it often says is that baptism is the first step of discipleship. I frequently taught this myself. But in recent years, I have come to discover that this is not exactly true. Discipleship, I believe, begins the moment we are born, when Jesus, through the work of the Holy Spirit, begins to draw us to Himself. As we age, we learn about God, sin, righteousness, and judgment in a myriad of different ways. We learn about these through nature, our conscience, and if we have access to it, through the Bible. All of this, strictly speaking, is discipleship, since we are learning about who we are and what God has done for us in Jesus Christ. Along the way, some of us hear specifically about Jesus and are persuaded to believe in Him for eternal life. Following this, we continue down the path of discipleship until we die.

In this way of thinking, discipleship is a life-long process; not something that begins once we believe. If you disagree, just remember that there were many disciples of Jesus in the Gospels who did not believe in Jesus for eternal life, many of whom followed for a while, but then turned back. The greatest example, of course, is Judas Iscariot himself. He was not only a disciple, a follower of Jesus, but was one of the twelve apostles. And yet Scripture implies that Judas never believed in Jesus and therefore, did not receive eternal life. Yet he was always a disciple.

So we must not say that baptism is the first step in discipleship. It isn't. If a person is baptized at all (more on that later), it is simply one of the many steps in a very long process. Remember, after all, that in New Testament times, water baptism was simply a public declaration that you were dying to your past and were making a fresh start for a new future. This technically could be done at any place along the path of discipleship, and could theoretically be done numerous times depending on the aspect of your life you were dying to.

Having said all this, however, it is nevertheless quite true that in the book of Acts, new converts to Christianity were often baptized in water quite soon after their conversion. This was not always the case (cf. Apollos in Acts 18:24–19:5), but is generally true. Aside from this, one of the main reasons people often think that baptism is a first step in discipleship is because of what Jesus says in Matthew 28:19-20.

People who speak and write about this verse often correctly note that the main verb in the passage is "make disciples" and all the other clauses explain *how*. This is true, especially if we remember that making disciples involves much more than just filling people's heads with Bible knowledge. Discipleship does not occur simply by reading all the latest theology books or by sitting in a pew and listening to a sermon.

The point, however, is that the phrase "baptizing them" partly explains *how* to make disciples. Matthew 28:19 says, "baptizing them in the name of the Father, the Son, and the Holy Spirit." Since this is the statement that immediately follows the main command to "make disciples" people assume this means that the first step in making a disciple is getting them baptized.

Now that we have learned something about the meaning of the word "baptism," is this really what Jesus is saying? Remember, whenever we see the word "baptism" in Scripture, we must not immediately think about dunking somebody under water, but must first remember what the word means, namely, "to be immersed, overcome, or fully identified with" something or somebody else. Then, with this definition in mind, we must read the verse again.

> *Go, therefore and make disciples of all the nations, immersing them and fully identifying them with the name of the Father, and of the Son, and of the Holy Spirit, teaching them to observe all things I have commanded you...*

With such a reading, water baptism may not be in view at all! To the contrary, the phrase "baptizing them in the name of the Father and of the Son and of the Holy Spirit" may just be another way of saying, "teaching them fully about the Father, the Son, and the Holy Spirit, helping them understand who God is and how to live more like God in our lives." With this reading, someone who is "baptized in the name of the Father, Son, and Holy Spirit" has become fully identified with the Trinitarian God, so that when people see us, they see God. In other words, since Jesus revealed God to us, a fully trained disciple is someone who looks and acts like Jesus to others. Such a person could be said to have been "baptized" or "immersed" or "fully identified with" Jesus.

When read this way, the first part of verse 20 where Jesus talks about teaching others is not a "second step" to discipleship, so that first you get baptized, and secondly you get taught. The phrase "baptizing them in the name of the Father, the Son, and the Holy Spirit" is another way of saying "teaching them to observe all that I have commanded you."

With such a reading, Matthew 28:19-20 becomes a classic case of Hebrew parallelism. The second statement does not follow the other sequentially, but amplifies and further explains the first statement. Such a way of teaching is somewhat foreign to our logic-driven, outline-focused, step-centered Western way of thinking, but was one of the primary ways Middle Eastern teachers and thinkers taught in Biblical times. And lest we forget, Jesus was a Jewish Rabbi.

If you are still not convinced of this perspective, assume for a moment that the "traditional" reading is right, and that Jesus was teaching the apostles how new converts should be immersed under water as soon as possible, and that this baptism should be done in the name of the Father, and of the Son, and of the Holy Spirit. This is an easy assumption, since this is how most baptisms are performed today. When I was baptized as a teenager, my father (who is a pastor), before he plunged me under the water, said these words: "Jeremy, based on your confession of faith in the Lord Jesus Christ, I now baptize you in the name of the Father, and of the Son, and of the Holy Spirit." *Sploosh!*

When I was a pastor, this is how I baptized everybody as well. It is a common formula and most of us are familiar with it.

Yet I think that if one of the apostles were present at such a baptism, they would tilt their head quizzically and say, "I know

I've been dead for almost 2000 years, so please forgive my ignorance … but why are you baptizing someone in the name of the Father, and of the Son, and of the Holy Spirit? The Son, Jesus, I understand. He died and rose for us, and baptism represents that. But why the Father and the Holy Spirit? Neither one died or rose. Why are you baptizing in their name also?"

We would stare back at them and say, "Weren't you there when Jesus told you to do it this way? Isn't this how you baptized also?"

This apostle would respond, "Of course not. Haven't you read the book of Acts?"

Then we would begin to mentally go through the book of Acts, and much to our surprise, we would discover that of all the instances of people receiving water baptism in Acts, there is not a single case where an apostle baptizes someone "in the name of the Father, and the Son, and the Holy Spirit." Every single time, without fail, the person is baptized into Jesus Christ (cf. Acts 2:38; 8:12, 16; 10:48; 19:5). This makes sense, of course, because this is, after all, what water baptism represents. Water baptism symbolizes our complete identification with Jesus in His death, burial, and resurrection.

So if Jesus was truly talking about water baptism in Matthew 28:19-20, then why is it that there is not a single example in all of Scripture where someone receives water baptism according to the "formula" of Matthew 28:19? This question has caused much controversy in the church, but the simple solution is to see that Matthew 28:19 is not a baptismal formula at all. When Jesus instructs the disciples to go and make other disciples, they already knew what discipleship meant, because they had just been with

Jesus for three years and had learned first-hand how to make disciples. And remember, Jesus did not "baptize" a single one of them (cf. John 4:1-2). But Jesus did teach them how to show love, forgiveness, grace, and mercy to all.

Now, in Matthew 28:19-20, before Jesus leaves, He tells His disciples to pick up where He left off, and do for others what He has done for them. In the same way He taught them, they must now teach others. They should train disciples in the way that He trained them. They should teach, show, and help others to understand what God is like, what Jesus is like, and what the Holy Spirit is like. They must live in the power and presence of all three members of the Trinity, revealing God to the world just as Jesus had revealed God to them. This is the message of Matthew 28:19-20, and there is not a drop of water in sight.

We have already seen that the Book of Acts supports this view in that the apostles nowhere baptized people "in the name of the Father, the Son, and the Holy Spirit," but let us turn to the Book of Acts to see if we can learn anything more about water baptism, and what it meant to the people at that time.

The Book of Acts

One difficulty with discussing baptism in the book of Acts is that the book refers to numerous different types of baptism. Take Acts 19:1-6 as an example. Within the span of six verses, three different types of baptism are mentioned, though in the passage, only two are called "baptism." There is the baptism of John (19:3-4), the baptism into Jesus Christ (19:5), and the baptism of the Holy Spirit (19:2, 6). This third type is not specifically called "baptism" in Acts 19, but other passages do refer to the coming of the Holy

Spirit as a baptism. So as we look at the subject of baptism in Acts, we must recall that not all references to "baptism" refer to dunking somebody under water.

Another curious aspect about baptism in the book of Acts is that the number and frequency of baptisms decreases as the book progresses. This decreasing emphasis on baptism continues throughout the rest of the New Testament, until at one point, Paul specifically declares that he is glad that he baptized so few people because God didn't send him to baptize, but to preach the gospel (1 Cor 1:14-17).[7] Paul elsewhere indicates that the real washing occurs with the water of the Word (Eph 5:26), and even Peter himself seems to disregard water baptism as having any real significance (cf. 1 Pet 3:21).

Why is there a decreasing emphasis on water baptism in Acts and the rest of the New Testament? It is possible, of course, that water baptism continued to be practiced as frequently as ever, and the writers simply stopped mentioning it. But when we understand the cultural and religious significance of water baptism in the first century Mediterranean world, and specifically the role of baptism within the book of Acts, it becomes clear that water baptism served a special and specific role within the early church which became unnecessary later on.

What then was the role and purpose of water baptism in the early church, and specifically in the book of Acts? Water baptism is a key indicator for *transitions* in Acts. Just as many modern

[7] Apollos may have carried out most of the water baptisms. See the possible word play in 1 Corinthians 3:6-8.

book and screenplay authors use water (e.g., with rain) to indicate that a change is coming in the plot, so also, the author of the Book of Acts used baptism to indicate a transition was occurring in his narrative. Each reference to water baptism indicates that the gospel of the Kingdom of God has arrived to a new people group. The gospel is first presented to the Jews in Jerusalem, and upon receiving it, they also get baptized (Acts 2). From there, the gospel spreads to the outcast, half-breed Samaritans, who also get baptized (Acts 8), until finally, the gospel is preached to the despised Gentiles who get baptized (Acts 10–11). Eventually, the gospel spreads to the entire world, even to those who were traditionally despised and rejected, such as women and enemy Roman soldiers (Acts 16, 19), who receive baptism upon believing.

In the cases where the gospel is presented to the different ethnic groups, it is Peter who goes and uses the "Keys of the Kingdom" to unlock the door of the gospel to a people group that was previously cut off from God and the gospel (cf. Matt 16:19; Eph 2:11-18). Paul, as the apostle to the Gentiles, is the one who allows Gentile women and Roman soldiers to hear the gospel and be baptized. In this way, Acts uses baptism to show the advancement of the kingdom to include all people who were formally shut out and cut off. Acts shows that the dividing wall of hostility has been torn down. The barrier is no more.

As a side note, it is important also to note what happens with Spirit baptism in the Book of Acts. Every time the gospel is preached to a new segment of humanity, Spirit baptism accompanies water baptism. That is, early in the Book of Acts, when the gospel is preached to a new group of people, those who believe in Jesus typically do not receive the Holy Spirit until they are baptized in water. When they receive the Spirit, the coming of the Holy Spirit with signs and wonders is the outward proof to Peter that God truly has accepted this new group of people into the family of God. But after this initial preaching of the gospel to these various groups, the baptism of the Spirit comes immediately upon a person who believes in Jesus for eternal life, whether or not they are baptized in water. Furthermore, these later occurrences of Spirit baptism are no longer accompanied by signs and wonders. So again, this is evidence of the transitionary nature of the Book of Acts. The gospel preaching of Peter initially opened the door to the Jews, the Samaritans, and the Gentiles, but once it is opened, no more physical manifestations of the baptism of the Holy Spirit were necessary to prove that God had indeed accepted a new group of people into His family.

In the case of water baptism, every single instance in the Book of Acts appears to follow the widely practiced method of immersion under water which was practiced by nearly every religion of that time. But it is the symbolism that is important. In every religion, including Judaism, water baptism symbolized the loss of the person's previous identity, and the birth of a new identity. Water baptism represented a death to the past and a new life for the future. Since nearly every religion practiced this, everyone knew what it meant. So when the news spread that a person had been baptized, their family, friends, and neighbors would ask why they had been baptized, what their new identity was going to be, and how their life would look in the future. And then, of course, they would watch to see if these changes truly took place.

In the case of new converts to Christianity being baptized into Jesus Christ, the new believers would explain to their inquiring friends and family who Jesus was, what He taught, and what had happened to Him in His death and resurrection. The new convert would say that now that they had fully identified themselves with Jesus through baptism, they were going to try to live their life in a way that reflected His teachings, His values, and His life.

However, there is one passage in the book of Acts that initially seems to challenge the idea that baptisms were intended to be a public demonstration of a life-changing decision which would cause others to ask the baptized person about what they had changed. This is the passage about the Ethiopian Eunuch in Acts 8:26-40.

According to Acts 8:27, this Ethiopian was a Eunuch of great authority under Candace, the Queen of Ethiopia. He had charge over the entire royal treasury, which indicates he was a high-ranking public official in the royal courts of Ethiopia.

As the account unfolds, the deacon Philip is walking along a road and overhears the Eunuch reading from Isaiah and offers to explain the Scripture to him. After doing so, the man believes in Jesus, and Philip takes him down to some nearby water to baptize him. Note that if this man was a proselyte to Judaism, as the text hints that he was (cf. 8:27), he would have already been baptized into Judaism. Now he was getting baptized again, this time into a full identification with Jesus Christ.

But the question is this: How could this have been a public identification with Jesus if nobody witnessed the baptism except for Philip? The way this passage is usually presented in sermons and drawings is that Philip and the Eunuch are all alone on a deserted road, and the two of them go down into the water to be baptized. If this Ethiopian Eunuch was all alone and far away from home, then nobody would have seen or known what he did on this deserted road in Israel, and therefore, his baptism could not have been a public testimony to anyone.

Yet a moment's reflection allows us realize that this Eunuch was probably not alone. After all, he was a powerful public official in Ethiopia, overseeing the entire treasury. It is quite certain that he was traveling with an entire retinue of servants and body guards. There is even a hint of this in the text where we are told that he was sitting in the chariot reading Isaiah while someone else drove. When he wanted to get baptized, he commanded the chariot to stop (8:38). Clearly, there were others traveling with the Ethiopian Eunuch who would have seen him get baptized, would have asked him about it on their journey back to Ethiopia, and would have observed his life and actions to see what differences (if any) followed as a result of the Eunuch fully identifying himself with Jesus.

So this baptism also was a public declaration by the Ethiopian Eunuch that he was making a drastic change in his life by dying to his past, and was fully identifying himself with the life and example of Jesus Christ.

Romans 6

Romans 6 may be the most famous passage in the Bible about baptism. It is this chapter which is most often preached at baptismal services, and these are the Scriptures people go to when they want to talk about the symbolism, necessity, and power of baptism. During baptismal classes, it is this passage that pastors use to explain the meaning and significance of baptism. This is for good reason, since Romans 6 does contain some great truths about baptism.

The problem is that Romans 6 is not exactly about water baptism. It is primarily about Spirit baptism. We know this because water baptism does not result in dying with Christ (6:4), and the parallel passage in Colossians 2:11-12 compares spiritual circumcision with spiritual baptism.

Furthermore, the flow of argument in Paul's letter shows that he has Spirit baptism in mind, rather than water baptism. In Romans 4–5, Paul goes into great detail about how a person is justified before God. Justification, he says, is by faith alone, apart from works of any kind (cf. Rom 4:4-5; 5:1, 21).

Then in Romans 6, Paul writes about what our justification means in real life. He continues this discussion all the way through chapter 8. The overall context of Romans 6–8 emphasizes the spiritual benefits of being identified with Christ. Paul's ultimate point in these chapters is that we have been completely freed from sin and the law through the Spirit. When we believe in Jesus for eternal life, the Holy Spirit places us "in Jesus Christ" so that we live with Him, die with Him, and are raised to new life with Him. Being washed with water is not what accomplishes this, but rather, it is being fully identified with the life, death, and resurrection of Jesus through the work of the Spirit that gives us this freedom from sin and the law.

This point becomes much clearer in Romans 6 if we remember that "baptism" means "immersion into" or "fully identified with." With this in mind, Romans 6:2-4 could be read this way:

How shall we who died to sin live any longer in it? Or do you not know that as many of us as were fully identified with Jesus Christ were fully identified with His death? Therefore we were buried with Him through being fully identified with death, that just as Christ was raised from the dead by the glory of the Father, even so we should walk in newness of life.

It seems clear from such a reading that Paul is talking primarily about what the Spirit does for those who believe. Paul would probably hasten to add that although it is the Holy Spirit who accomplishes this complete identification with Jesus, it is helpful to provide an outward symbol of this inner reality by undergoing water baptism. This would then enable those who believed with a natural opportunity to explain to friends and family what had happened to them.

Summary of Baptism Symbolism

This brief survey of Scriptures on baptism has revealed that water baptism was a symbolic ritual in biblical times which everybody understood, even those who were not followers of Jesus. It was practiced in nearly every culture and every religion of the first century Mediterranean world, and symbolized death to the past and full identification with a new way of living for the future. Sometimes people were baptized once in a lifetime; some multiple times.

The key to the Christian use of baptism, however, was that because the symbolism was so widely used and recognized, when someone received baptism, their friends, family, and coworkers would ask them what they were dying to, what their future life would look like, and why they were making this drastic change. These questions enabled the early Christians to use baptism as a way to share about Jesus with their friends, family, neighbors, and coworkers.

So the question for us today is this: Does water baptism share the same universal symbolism that it did in the days of Jesus and the apostles? If not, is water baptism still required today? Is there some other symbolic ritual that might accomplish the same purpose as baptism, but which is more universally recognized?

It is to these questions we now turn.

BAPTISM TODAY

Since baptism was a widely-practiced religious and cultural symbol of the first century Mediterranean world, if believers today truly want to follow the example of the early church in "baptizing" new converts, it may be best to seek a modern cultural equivalent to baptism, rather than woodenly use a symbol from 2000 years ago that has lost most of its natural significance and meaning. In other words, just as the modern equivalent to washing someone's feet might be washing someone's toilet, so also, if we really wanted to practice modern-day baptism, it may be best to find a modern cultural parallel to what water baptism meant in the days of the early church, and then use that modern practice instead.

Nevertheless, before we get to possible modern parallels, it is important to point out three reasons why it may be best to simply continue the rite of water baptism "the way it has always been done." First, water baptism is a traditional church practice. Water baptism is what Jesus and the apostles practiced, and what nearly all believers have undergone during the past 2000 years of church history. For this reason, and this reason alone, it is never *wrong* for a person to receive water baptism, especially if those who undergo it and those who observe it are instructed in the symbolism of baptism.

After all, the symbolism in water baptism is very strong. This is the second reason we could choose to simply maintain the practice of water baptism today. Though alternatives will be suggested below, some may decide that there is no better symbolic ritual which so wonderfully depicts the idea of being buried with Christ and being raised to a new life in Him. Water baptism is like a visual sermon. It tells the story of Jesus' death and resurrection and our full participation with Him. This is one reason I am somewhat opposed to the idea of sprinkling as a mode of baptism. Sprinkling with water does not so clearly depict our burial and resurrection with Jesus as does immersion.

Third, just as numerous religions in the days of Jesus and the apostles practiced various forms of baptism and ritual washings, the same is true today. Numerous religions still practice ritual washings and baptisms by which they symbolically cleanse themselves in water. Hindus immerse themselves in the Ganges River, Orthodox Jews undergo annual Mikvah, and Muslims perform various ritualistic washings for themselves and for the dead.

And yet these same three reasons to continue water baptism today are also three reasons why water baptism could cease. Traditions are wonderful, but over time, traditions often lose their meaning and significance until we perform them simply because we always have. I fear that this is exactly what has happened to baptism.

While the deep symbolism of baptism is still present in the

ritual, it is not naturally understood or comprehended by the average Christian, let alone the person who knows little about Jesus and Scripture. Originally, the symbolism of baptism was immediately and universally understood. That is what made it so powerful when adopted and adapted by the early church. But today, we have to explain the symbolism to everybody, which causes the symbol to lose its natural significance.

The fact that other religions practice forms of baptism and ritualistic washings muddies the water even more. In most other religions, the baptism or ritualistic washing is required as a way to approach their god. Failing to do so may result in strict and severe punishment. In these other religions, it is taught that water baptism actually spiritually cleanses and purifies the person. But this is not true in Christianity. In fact, the opposite is true. For the Christian, baptism does nothing for the soul or spirit, but simply gets the skin wet. It is a washing of the body, and nothing else. It removes dirt from the flesh, but does nothing to remove the stain of sin on the soul (1 Pet 3:21). For spiritual cleansing, we look to Jesus Christ alone. We believe in Jesus for His righteousness. Sadly, far too many Christians do not realize this basic fact, and believe that our God is like the gods of these other religions, and is pleased and appeased through water baptism. It is sometimes taught that if a new believer does not receive water baptism, God will be angry with them, will not bless them, and may not give them eternal life. Some of this, I fear, is due to the influence of religions like Hinduism, Judaism, and Islam which are based on works, rather than on faith, and so maintaining a practice which reinforces this idea is more harmful than it is helpful.

So the main reasons to keep baptism around are also reasons

to give up the rite of baptism. But this does not mean we give up the *symbolism* altogether. There are numerous modern equivalents to baptism which have the same significance, but which do not carry all the traditional and religious baggage. I am all in favor of having an outward symbol which reflects the inner spiritual change. As mentioned earlier, symbols are like visual sermons, and we need more of them. But for symbols to work, they have to be immediately understood by those in the surrounding culture.

Just as a joke loses its humor when it has to be explained, so also a symbol loses its force when it needs explaining. Though water baptism is a great and wonderful symbol, it is not immediately understood by our surrounding culture as it was in New Testament times. Today, most people (including most Christians) just think it is some slightly odd religious ritual that we do for the sake of tradition. And for most, that is exactly what it has become.

Death Rites

The rite of baptism needs to die and be raised again to new life in the form of new symbols. We need modern symbols that represent what baptism represented in New Testament times, so that when people see us do these things, they immediately understand that something has changed in our life and ask us what has happened. The symbol, whatever it is, needs to indicate a fresh start, a new beginning, a rebirth.

The symbol should also be public, not just with people who agree with you in beliefs and behavior, but among and in the midst of those who, when they see what you are doing, will ask, "Why did you do that? What change has occurred in your life?" It should be a conversation starter so that the person who performed this action can explain to their friends and family what they have learned about Jesus, and how their life will be different as a result.

The symbols should represent a break with the past and the beginning of a new future. If possible, it would also be good to symbolize death, burial, and resurrection. One way to look for symbols is to look at the burial customs of a particular culture, and then try to find a ritual, ceremony, or symbol that mimics that burial custom.

As an example, there is group of people in the Philippines known as the Caviteño. When a Cavite person is nearing death due to sickness or old age, the person goes out into the forest and selects a tree. Then the family members build the person a little hut at the base of this tree in which they will live until they die. But they are not left alone to die. The family and friends come out to help the dying person hollow out the tree trunk of the standing tree. When the person dies, he or she is entombed vertically in the hollowed-out tree trunk. The symbolism is that just as trees give life to the tribe through fruit and wood for their fires, so when a person dies, they give their life back to the tree.

So in the Caviteño culture, a water baptism would not represent death, burial, and resurrection at all. But maybe when a Cavite chooses to leave their former way of life and turn to follow Jesus, it would be appropriate for them to go out into the woods and select a tree. Then, they inform their friends and relatives that they are going to go live in the hut, and they might ask their family members to help them hollow out the tree trunk. Then, on a certain day, they get into the tree trunk where they stay for a period of time, before returning back out of the tree, as through returning from the dead. Such actions would certainly cause everybody who heard of it and witnessed to ask why the person was acting like they were dying when in reality they were not. Such a custom would naturally enable this new believer to share about how they died with Christ, and in Him were given new life.

Or take a certain group of Tibetin Buddhists who practice "sky burial." When a person dies, the family hires a certain man of the town to go with them to a barren field outside of town. There, the man cuts the dead body into pieces and feeds it to the vultures. Once again, water baptism would be meaningless in such a culture. So rather than force new believers to undergo a meaningless ritual, it might be better to find a death and resurrection ritual that everybody would see and understand. Yet how might one symbolically give themselves a "sky burial"? This would be a task for the new Christians of that culture to decide for themselves. Maybe they could take some meat and present it to the vultures, or find some other symbolic gesture that would be immediately understood by others in that culture.

With some creative thinking, such symbolic rituals of death and resurrection could be performed in nearly all cultures for any burial ceremony. Some cultures wrap the body in cloth and dump it in the sea. In other cultures, bodies are sent down a river in a canoe, or floated out to sea on a raft, or raised up to the sky in the trees. While some of these rituals would be dangerous to do to an actual living person, maybe a replica of the person could be made out of wood or stone, and then dumped into the sea or sent down the river.

In western culture, there are two main customs on how to treat people who die: they are either buried or cremated. Water baptism is a decent picture of burial, but the image might be even better if the baptism ceremony looked more like a funeral. The baptismal candidates would not dress in the traditional white robes, but in formalwear instead, just like dead bodies are often prepared for burial. Also, the symbolism could be greatly enhanced if there was a burial procession on the way to the baptism, and if the baptismal tank looked less like a hot tub and more like a casket. Water may not even need to be used. These sorts of adjustments to the baptismal ceremony would make the death, burial, and resurrection symbolism much more obvious for the average viewer.

What might be really symbolic is to have an actual casket up on the stage, and have the baptismal candidate lay down in it in front of everyone. The lid is closed, and then after a short period, it is reopened, and to everyone's amazement, the body is gone! But then the person reappears at the back of the room and walks again to the front. This sort of thing is done all the time in magic shows, and while I don't know how the magicians do it, if a church could pull this off, it would do a wonderful job symbolizing the death, burial, and miraculous resurrection of those who believe in Jesus for eternal life. The danger with such an idea is that the ceremony becomes more of a magic show than a symbol of a life-changing event. But then, most baptismal ceremonies today are little more than magical rites and shows anyway.

Cremation might be much more difficult. Safely symbolizing cremation would require creative thinking. But again, maybe someone could make a replica of themselves out of wood or straw, and then dress it in their clothes, and in front of everyone, burn the replica on a funeral pyre. When the fire dies, the ashes could then be collected and scattered in some important location. These are just a few examples of symbolic rituals that could be adopted today in lieu of water baptism. Such symbolic rituals would naturally inform the observers what the person was claiming about themselves: that the old person had died and was gone, and a new person had risen from the dead. These alternative rituals might do a better job of representing our death, burial, and resurrection with Jesus, and when we undergo them, might cause people who know us and observe what we are doing, to ask us why we would undergo such a bizarre and morbid ceremony. Such ceremonies could still be called "baptisms" for they are still symbolic representations of our identification with and full immersion into the life, death, burial, and resurrection of Jesus Christ.

Changing Rites

Death and burial rites are not the only possibilities for representing a break with the past and a change for a new life in the future. Our culture is full of other symbolic gestures for showing such a break. None of these following symbols have quite the same power and force as water baptism might have had in New Testament times or as some of the replacements from today suggested above, but in many ways, they might be more effective today than water baptism at sparking conversations with friends and family about the changes that are being made in the life of the new believer.

Cut Your Hair. I have long hair. Honestly, it is not because I like long hair. I find long hair to be rather annoying. But I grew my hair out for symbolic reasons which have to do with my job as a prison chaplain. First, although I am a prison chaplain, I am a correctional worker first, and am there to protect and serve the community by helping maintain the safe and orderly operation of the prison. And yet, as a follower of Jesus, I wanted to show the men at the prison that I was not just another prison guard. I was different. Most of the prison guards have military backgrounds, and the military haircut to go with it. By growing my hair out, I visually set myself apart from the other prison employees, even though I was one of them.

Ironically, in the process of growing my hair out, I soon found that the people who judged me for it the most were the incarcerated men. I cannot tell you how many times I have had a man come up to me after a Bible Study or a church service in prison, asking to speak to me in private. When we get back to my office, they pull out their Bible and tell me that God has given them a verse for me. Then they read 1 Corinthians 11:14: "Does not even nature itself teach you that if a man has long hair, it is a dishonor to him?" I once had a man misquote the verse and change "dishonor" into "abomination" but that is beside the point. The first time this happened, I had a little debate there in my office about using proper historical-cultural hermeneutics to interpret Scripture, but over the years, I have finally settled on a simpler answer. I say, "That is exactly why I wear it long. I want to be shamed." They usually don't know what to say to this, and the conversation ends. But after this happened a few times, I realized that my long hair was also a symbol in another way: not only did it show everybody that I was somehow different than the militaristic prison guard, but I was also different than the legalistic religious Christian. In prison, almost everybody is a legalist.

About two years into my job, I got tired of the long hair and cut it. That was when I realized that cutting long hair really can be like baptism in New Testament times. Everybody who knows you sees that you cut your long hair and asks why you did it. To my shame (real shame, this time), I had no good reason. A few months later, two female staff members also cut their long hair. When I noticed, I asked them why they did it. They had good answers: They were donating their hair to "Locks of Love," an organization that provides wigs to children who are undergoing chemotherapy for cancer. Later, a Native American inmate at the prison cut off his long hair, and when I asked him why, he said it was because a family member died, and this was one of their cultural ways of mourning.

Cutting off long hair invites people to ask why it was done, and what has changed in your life. Even if you don't have long hair, you can grow it out for a period of time, and then cut it. People will notice the change both ways. Men could even do this with their facial hair if that is preferred. One of the prison guards I work with recently started growing out his beard. I asked him why, and he told me about something in his life that he was trying to change, and said that when it finally changed, he was going to cut his beard. He recently cut his beard, and when I saw him at work, I immediately knew what had happened in his life and was able to congratulate him on the change.

Growing and cutting hair even has biblical precedent in the vows of the Nazarites. Nazarite vows were usually for a short period of time, during which time the hair would not be cut (Numbers 6). When the vow was complete, the person would cut their hair, symbolizing the change that occurred. Samson, of course, was a lifelong Nazarite, and when his hair was finally cut, it truly did represent his death (Judg 16:19-22).

The point is that the growing and cutting of hair is very symbolic in our culture. Doing this will generate questions about what happened and why it was done, just as water baptism generated these questions in biblical times. If a new believer gets baptized today, almost nobody will ask why. Most of those outside the church will not even know it happened. But if a new believer cuts their long hair, they must be ready to give an answer to those who ask why. People will want to know what changed in their life. These sorts of questions provide great opportunities for the new believer to explain that they are now a follower of Jesus and the cutting of hair was a symbolic way of representing this change.

There are numerous other cultural rituals and symbols which could be used to indicate that a change has taken place, and which would cause people to ask why this ritual was undertaken. Any visible, outward, public display which would cause people to ask what it represented could accomplish the same purpose that water baptism accomplished in New Testament times. Water baptism indicated a death to the past and a new life for the future. So in our society, any action that indicates such a radical change could be seen as a form of culturally relevant baptism.

I have a friend who always wears black. All black, all the time. She is not gothic; she just likes black. One day she came in wearing a pink shirt. It was shocking. And of course, she got asked why. In the opposite way, if someone wears colorful clothing, and then starts wearing all white, or all black, people will ask why.

Changing your name might also be a way to indicate a break with the past. It is a symbol that often accompanies marriage or a change in religion. People sometimes change their names when they become Muslim or Jewish; why not change your name if you become a follower of Jesus?

In a materialistic culture like ours where everyone is striving for more money, bigger houses, and nicer cars, one way to symbolize a change would be to downsize to a smaller house and an old beater of a car. Such actions in our culture seem crazy and foolish, and are sure to generate questions about what happened and why you did it.

Earlier we looked at the cutting of hair, and noted that it has biblical precedent in the vow of the Nazarites. The Nazarite vow also included not touching dead animals and not drinking wine. If someone today stopped eating meat and stopped drinking wine and beer, this might cause people who knew them to ask why, depending on who their friends were.

In other circles, body piercings or getting a tattoo (or having one removed) might be appropriate. Without fail, when people get tattoos today, friends, family, and coworkers who see it say, "Nice tat! What does it mean?" Such questions naturally provide opportunities for the new believer to share with others the change that has come about in their life.

I have a friend who recently dropped over 20,000 people he followed on Twitter. He received hundreds of Tweets and emails asking why he did it. It wasn't because he had recently become a follower of Jesus, but for some other reasons. Nevertheless, the response he received made me realize that dying to your Twitter followers is a technological form of baptism. It causes people to ask why you did it.

I know someone else who did this with his blog. His blog was very popular, and he had thousands of page views every day, and tens of thousands of backlinks. If you are a blogger, you know how difficult this is. A few years ago, he made a drastic change in his life, and to symbolize this change, he deleted his entire blog. People thought he was crazy to do such a thing. A top blog is hard to get. Why would anyone just delete it? If he didn't want it, he should sell it, or redirect the traffic to a different blog, but nobody just kills off a popular blog. But he did, and he got hundreds of people asking him why.

As you can see, when it comes to symbolizing change that has occurred in your life, there is almost no limit to the possibilities. Much of it depends on your own particular group of friends and what would cause them to ask what has changed in your life.

CONCLUSION

In biblical times, getting baptized was a public declaration that something drastic had changed in your life, and you were dying to the past and would now live differently in the future. People would not only ask what you had died to, but would also watch your life to see if any change was evident. Usually, water baptism does not evoke such questions today, even in church.

So maybe it is time for the rite of baptism to be baptized itself—for it to die and rise again in a way that is meaningful in our culture. If you want to get water baptized for tradition's sake, that is fine, but at least consider *also* performing some other sort of culturally relevant ritual or ceremony which indicates to others that a radical change has occurred in your life. Then people will ask what change you made, and why, and you will be able to tell them about your decision to follow the life and teachings of Jesus.

DISCUSSION QUESTIONS

1. Was John the Baptist the first person in history to start baptizing people in water as a symbol of their death to the past and their start of a new future? If not, where did John likely get this symbolic act?

2. What does the word "baptism" mean? Is baptism always done with water? What other methods of baptism are found in the Bible?

3. The baptism of Jesus, as well as most of the early baptisms in the Bible were for what "religion" (it's not Christianity)?

4. The baptism of John was a call for what? What sorts of things did the people who were baptized by John do after they were baptized?

5. Why did Jesus get baptized?

6. Explain Matthew 28:19-20 in light of the discussion about baptism found in this chapter. What do you think of this explanation? Does it help when you translate the Greek word *baptizō* instead of just leave

it transliterated as "baptize" as found in most English translations?

7. What is the role of baptism in the book of Acts?

8. Romans 6 discusses what form of baptism?

9. Several suggestions were made about some alternative symbols for personal change that are readily understood by most people today. What did you think of these alternatives? Can you think of any others? Do you think it would be good to use these instead of baptism to symbolize conversion? Why or why not?

CHAPTER 2

THE RITE OF COMMUNION

I sometimes think that one good indication of church theology gone awry is when the church cannot come to agreement on certain beliefs or behaviors. In other words, the existence of disunity is a sign that something is being misunderstood, and not just by one side or the other, but by all sides of the debate. I know this is a simplistic way of looking at things, but I sometimes think that if the various church groups and denominations could stop pointing fingers and condemning each other to hell long enough to come together and talk things through with kind words, clear minds, and an eye on the cultural and historical context of Scripture, a lot more unity might exist in the universal church today.

Take communion for example. Much like baptism, there is a wide variety of opinions on what communion (also known as the Eucharist) does, who can administer it, who can receive it, what it symbolizes, what elements should be used, and what happens to the elements when they are blessed and distributed. Specifically, does communion actually bestow grace and forgiveness upon those who receive it? Can grape juice be used, or must it be wine? If grape juice can be used, can other liquids as well? What about the bread? Does it have to be unleavened? Why? Can anybody give communion to anybody else, or must it be administered only by a member of the clergy, and only to people who are members of the church? And when the bread and wine are blessed, do they transform either spiritually or substantially into the blood and body of Jesus Christ, or do they simply remain bread and wine? There is even a controversy over what to call this "meal." Is it "communion," or "the Eucharist," or "the Lord's Supper"?

Do you see the controversies that surround this simple meal? I find it sadly ironic that one of the things which Jesus Christ gave His disciples as a way to encourage unity and "communion" with one another, has become one of the things that creates the most division and disunity within the church.

All of this division and disunity makes me wonder if we have all completely misunderstood what this "meal" is and how it is to be observed. I wonder if all of the things about this meal that cause division and strife could fade away into insignificance if we understood what the meal originally was, what it symbolized, and therefore, how we can practice it today.

This is why the Lord's Supper is the second religious rite which churches would be wise to give up. Not that we would actually get rid of it, but just as with baptism, we can look at the symbolism it had in the days of Jesus and the early church, and then find ways to resurrect and maintain that same symbolism today.

After stating some of the reservations I have with the Lord's Supper the way it is practiced today, this chapter will look at the biblical passages about the Lord's Supper, how the Lord's Supper transitioned into communion and the Eucharist, and will conclude with some brief suggestions for how the symbolism behind the Lord's Supper might better be accomplished today. In this way, we are not doing away with the Lord's Supper, but are allowing the way it is performed today to die a natural death so that it can be raised to new life and new meaning in the church today.

RESERVATIONS WITH THE LORD'S SUPPER

Just as with baptism, the typical communion service today borders on the mystical and magical. This is especially true in some Catholic and Lutheran circles where the bread and wine inherit the actual (or spiritual) attributes of the body and blood of Jesus. I have no intention or desire to delve into the debate surrounding consubstantiation (the Lutheran view) and transubstantiation (the Catholic view), except to say that both, in one way or another, see the bread and wine as becoming something more than just bread and wine, and in this way, the elements become holy and impart grace to the believer.

The whole debate about what happens to the bread and wine centers around the definition of the word "is" in Matthew 26:26, 28 (cf. Luke 22:19-20). Though often mocked for his statement, Bill Clinton was right: "It depends on what the meaning of the word 'is' is." Whether or not President Clinton was trying to be tricky with that statement, it is nevertheless quite true, especially when we consider the words of Jesus at the Last Supper. What did He mean when He said "This *is* my body … This *is* my blood"? Well, it all depends on what the meaning of the word "is" is. Protestants say Jesus was using the word "is" to describe a metaphor or symbol. Lutherans say Jesus was talking literally, but in a spiritual way. Catholics are the most literal of all, and say that the bread and wine actually become the body and blood of Jesus.

I, of course, being an evangelical Christian, take the Protestant position, and yet I think that in so doing, we have not avoided the problems surrounding the Lord's Supper, but only intensified them. Though the Protestant church tradition has stripped away most of the mystical significance of the elements, they still practice communion in a way that is almost identical to those who maintain the mystical elements, which makes the Lord's Supper not more meaningful, but less.

This brings us back to the problem of communion itself. As indicated at the beginning of this chapter, the fact that there is a debate of this magnitude over something which was supposed to create unity within the Body of Christ indicates that everybody on all sides of the debate share in a basic misunderstanding about this meal. The debate is solved, not by trying to figure out which side is right and which is wrong, but by finding the foundational and faulty premise which all the perspectives have in common. If this is fixed, the division and strife fades away, and unity naturally develops.

When it comes to the division of the Lord's Supper, it seems that when we understand the symbolism of what Jesus is saying and doing in this Last Supper with His apostles, it is then that we see the true significance of His actions, and the debate about what happens (if anything) to the bread and wine fades away into irrelevance. Let us begin with where we are at today.

The observable practice of communion (or the Lord's Supper or the Eucharist) are all pretty similar no matter which church denomination or tradition is considered. Typically, a pastor or a priest reads a few Scriptures and says a few prayers over a bit of bread and wine, and then distributes these bits of bread and wine to those who have gathered. The whole ceremony is usually quite somber and reflective.

In other words, if you took an outsider and asked them to observe the communion practices of a Baptist church and a Lutheran church, they would be hard pressed to discern any real outward difference. Sure, there might be a few minor differences on where and how people get the bread and wine, what words the pastor or priest says over the elements, and a few other items, but for the most part, the practices are all quite similar. Since this is the case, what we are really arguing about?

Maybe despite all our theological differences, the *practical* differences are really not that far apart. Even if this is so, I will argue below that both theologically and practically, we may be light years away from what the Lord's Supper is really all about.

To see this, let us turn to look at a few key passages in Scripture which talk about the Lord's Supper so that we can understand what the meal was about, what it came to mean, and why it developed into such a significant symbol in the life of the early church.

THE LORD'S SUPPER IN BIBLE TIMES

Surprisingly few Christians realize that the first "Lord's Supper" was actually a Jewish Passover meal (cf. Matt 26:17-30; Luke 22:7-23). Jesus did not institute, invent, or create the Lord's Supper, but was instead observing the traditional Jewish meal with His disciples. Of course, even though Jesus did not institute this meal, He did instill it with new meaning and significance. Though the meal was traditional, He pointed the symbols and significance of the meal to Himself.

A typical Jewish Passover meal involves lots of food and wine, with numerous symbolic items and actions during the meal. The entire meal is designed to remind the Jewish people of the 400 years they spent in slavery in Egypt and how God miraculously delivered them through the help of Moses and the Ten Plagues. In the Jewish Passover meal, there are typically four cups of wine, each with its own name and meaning. There is unleavened bread, which reminds the Jews of the hurried nature of the original meal, and how they could not wait for the bread to rise. They eat horse-radish to remind them of the bitterness of slavery, herbs dipped in salt-water to remind them of the tears. There is lamb, to remind them of the lamb that was slain to put blood on the doorposts of their house. All of this commemorates the deliverance of Israel from slavery in Egypt.

The meal which Jesus shared with His disciples was probably quite similar to the way the meal is observed in Jewish homes to-day, except with one main difference. The gospel accounts indicate that Jesus turned the symbolism of the wine and the unleavened bread to point to Himself (Matt 26:17-30; Luke 22:7-23). One wonders if Jesus did this with the rest of the items in the meal as well.

Why did Jesus point the meal to Himself? It was not so that He could have some cool object lesson to illustrate His point, nor was it to show that the elements of the Passover meal were prophetically pointing to Him. Jesus might have been doing these things, but they were not His primary purpose. Instead, by pointing the Passover meal to Himself, Jesus sought to show His disciples that in Him, the entire world was delivered from slavery to sin and death. Just as Israel had been delivered from slavery to Egypt in the first Passover, now, in Jesus, a worldwide Passover was occurring for the deliverance of all people.

At that last meal, as Jesus said that the meal was being fulfilled in Him, the apostles would have thought back to the Exodus from Egypt, and how God had led His people forth in power to gain victory over the Egyptians through signs, wonders, and miracles. They would have assumed that similar things were about to happen to the people of Israel as Jesus led them to victory against the Roman Empire.

This did not happen, however. Instead, Jesus Himself was arrested, condemned, and crucified as a common criminal. Only after the resurrection did the apostles come to realize that the common enemy from which they, and all people of the earth were being delivered, was not the Romans, but sin, death, and the devil. These early Christians came to realize that in Jesus, even the Romans had been delivered. In Jesus, a universal Exodus was taking place. We see this idea develop as the church is born and the followers of Jesus begin to work out for themselves what it means to follow Jesus in their culture.

After Jesus observed His Last Supper with His disciples in the upper room, there is no further example in the final chapters of the Gospels or in the Book of Acts of this sort of meal happening again. Though some people point to texts like Acts 2:42 and 20:7 which talk about the "breaking of bread," these verses do not refer to the Passover meal, but to shared communal meals. The church gathered on a daily or weekly basis to eat meals together and discuss the things they were learning about following Jesus. But these were not Passover meals. They were just regular, everyday meals, in which people were gathering together to share food and fellowship.

By the time Paul writes 1 Corinthians, it appears that the believers in Corinth are gathering on a weekly basis to share a meal together, and they are calling it "the Lord's Supper" (1 Cor 11:20). There were problems with the way they were conducting this meal, and so Paul provides some corrective instruction about this meal (1 Cor 11:17-34). As part of these instructions, Paul refers to the Passover meal which Jesus shared with His disciples on the night before He was crucified (1 Cor 11:23-26). So in the span of a few decades, the "Lord's Supper" went from referring to the once-a-year observance of Passover in which Jesus pointed the elements of the meal to Himself, to referring instead to a more frequent meal of fellowship with other believers.

Yet if there is one thing that is clear from the accounts in Acts and the description in 1 Corinthians 11, the Lord's Supper was a full meal. In Corinth, the problem with the Lord's Supper was that some people were eating and drinking everything before everyone had arrived (1 Cor 11:21-22, 33-34). Some people were even getting drunk (1 Cor 11:21). Paul instructs them to wait for one another, so that everyone can share in the food and drink, and if there are some who are too hungry to wait, then they should eat a little bit at home before they come to the Lord's Supper so that it can be observed and enjoyed with everyone present (1 Cor 11:34).

From this description in 1 Corinthians 11, it appears that the Lord's Supper was a time for Christians to gather with one another over an actual meal, where they would enjoy conversation and fellowship with one another. Though the meal could literally have been Christians gathering to enjoy a meal together, it is possible that the meal included a short reminder about the death of Jesus. The symbolism in the bread and wine reminded the people about the broken body of Jesus and His blood shed for us. What He did on the cross invites Christians to live in unity with one another. There might also have been a time of more formal teaching and discussion about the Scriptures and what they taught about Jesus, and what it meant to be one of His followers (cf. Acts 20:7).

So how did the early church transition from a once-a-year observance of the Passover meal to a daily or weekly time of gathering for food and fellowship? In other words, how did the church take the words of Jesus as a Passover supper when He said, "Do this in remembrance of me?" and apply it to a weekly meal?

There were numerous factors that led to this transition. The first factor was cultural. Every culture around the world and throughout time has placed food near the center of their customs, traditions, and celebrations. Most cultures have noticed as well that relationships are best built over food. It is around the table that friendships are born, marriages are strengthened, and families are united. It is in the activity of eating food with others that traditions are passed down, stories are told, customs are affirmed, and values are endorsed. As a result, there are few activities that build community better than sharing a meal.

This was just as true in Roman, Greek, and Middle Eastern cultures as it is today. In fact, one of the central practices and customs of Middle Eastern culture was fellowship and discussion around meals (cf. Acts 2:42-46). All of this together made mealtime the perfect opportunity to teach and answer questions about Jesus, encourage one another to stand strong in the face of persecution, and simply share food and fellowship for the purpose of bonding and building relationships as was the custom.

Furthermore, the Passover meal was Jewish, and so it is likely that most Gentile believers rightly understood that as Gentiles, they did not have to observe Passover. Nevertheless, every culture has shared meals, and so they very likely followed the pattern Jesus had instituted at the Last Supper and incorporated this into their regular communal meals.

Ultimately then, the early church understood that when Jesus said, "Do this in remembrance of me," He wasn't referring to the bread and the wine, nor was He referring specifically to the Passover meal, or even a meal in general. Yes, the early church adopted a meal, but they were astute enough to know that the meal was not what was important; it is *what happens at a meal* that Jesus was referring to. Jesus had built a community of followers around Himself, and He wanted this community to continue. The early church knew that one of the best ways to build community was around the table. So they started sharing meals together on a regular basis, not because they had to for tradition's sake, or because Jesus had commanded them to (He really hadn't), but because they were family, they loved each other, and they liked hanging out with each other over a meal.

The second factor that led the early church to adopt a regular expression of the Lord's Supper in a meal is that it was practical. As we know from the Book of Acts and later church history, the early church struggled against threats from without and within. From the outside, they dealt with persecution from the Romans and the Jews. From the inside, the church stood up against false teaching about Jesus. Then, of course, there were all the new believers who needed to be welcomed into the family of God and taught the essentials of the faith.

In such a situation, the regular meeting of believers over a meal was the ideal place to build community, pass on instruction, and strengthen each other's' resolve about persecution. Even then, when people are simply gathering for a meal, it is difficult for the authorities to know whether they are simply friends, or if they are followers of Jesus. So meeting over a meal was the ideal way to accomplish all the basic goals and functions of the fledgling church.

Finally, and probably as a result of the previous two factors, there was a theological factor for why the early church practiced the Lord's Supper as a regular meal. Though everybody in Greco-Roman culture gathered regularly for meals, the new Christians began to recognize that in their meals, something new and exciting was occurring. They began to see that through a gathering of redeemed people, Jesus had also redeemed the meals of culture. Similarly, they began to see that Jesus had redeemed other things as well. In their midst, He was bringing redemption to the marriage bond, family structures, and even to the master-slave relationship (see Gal 3:28; Eph 2:14-18; 5:22–6:9).

As they met and discussed these things, they saw how Jesus fulfilled the Hebrew Scriptures, thereby redeeming them as well. They saw how Jesus defeated sin, death, and the devil, and all things that were in bondage to them, and in so doing, redeemed all things in Himself. Many of these new believers came to understand that the cross of Jesus was the central event in the history of the world. They began to filter all their beliefs and behaviors through the lens of Jesus Christ and Him crucified. This theological insight helped them see what sharing a regular meal could do for them as a new community on earth. The sharing of a meal became not just a way to eat food and share fellowship, but it became a theological symbol for what Jesus was doing for all people on earth, and eventually, finally, for the entire universe as well (1 Cor 15:20-28).

Since the death and resurrection of Jesus was central to Christian belief and practice, and since teaching was often done with the help of symbols, it became customary as a part of nearly every meal where Christians were gathered to remind people that the bread they were eating represented the body of Jesus which was broken for them, and the wine they were drinking represented His blood. By the time Paul writes 1 Corinthians, it appears that the tradition was firmly established that part of the meal of fellowship between believers included remembering the death of Jesus as symbolized by bread and wine.

The Scriptures, then, appear to paint a far different picture about the Lord's Supper than what is typically practiced in the average church today. The Lord's Supper was a weekly (or possibly more frequent) gathering of believers to enjoy a meal with each other. This would be a celebratory meal, where they would laugh, tell stories, and build relationships. There would probably be a formal time where someone reminded the people who had gathered of the basis and reason for their gathering, namely, Jesus. It was also likely that there was a time of formal teaching or discussion as part of the meal (cf. 1 Corinthians 12–14). This was the Lord's Supper, and it is also likely that this was the primary weekly gathering of the local church. It is also quite likely that this time consisted mostly of friends just sitting around talking and laughing together, as Jesus often did with His disciples.

So how did we get to where we are today? How did the church go from meeting weekly for full meals, fellowship, and celebration, to simply sharing a little bread and juice in five minutes at the end of a church service? How did this transition occur? How did the Lord's Supper become a religious rite?

THE RITE OF THE LORD'S SUPPER

It is plainly true that the Lord's Supper not only went through numerous transitions during the first several decades of the church, but had experienced even more transitions in the 2000 years since. The way the Lord's Supper is normally observed to-day, bears almost no resemblance to the way it was originally done by Jesus, or to the way it was modified by many of the early Christians. Jesus was observing a Passover meal and pointing the elements of the meal to Himself; the early church was sharing in the fellowship and community they had as followers of Jesus around the social glue of shared meals.

So how did we get to where we are today? How did the church go from sharing a full meal on a regular basis to eating a cracker and a teaspoon of wine at the end of a church service? Not surprisingly, the evolution of the Lord's Supper very closely matches the evolution of baptism. Just as baptism, over the course of hundreds of years and as a result of practical concerns and the-ological inquiry, went from immersing people under water to putting a few drops of water on people's heads (in some traditions), so also, the practice of the Lord's Supper evolved into its current form over time as a result of the practical needs and theological questions of the church.

First, some of the early changes were simply practical. After the closing of the Book of Acts, the early church faced intense and severe persecution for a couple hundred years. Many Christians were put into prison, and many more lost their jobs and faced constant threat of starvation. In this situation, it was impossible to regularly share a meal with others. When food could be brought to those in prison, the "Lord's Supper" often had to be celebrated quickly and furtively so as not to raise the ire or suspicion of the guards. In these cases, only the smallest portions of the essential "items" were shared—the bread and wine—for they reminded the believers most clearly about the body and blood of Jesus.

The second reason for the shift was political. In the early fourth century A. D., Emperor Constantine converted to Christianity, and in so doing, made Christianity the official religion of the Roman Empire. Not wanting to be on the "wrong side" of the Emperor, many priests who formerly practiced some form of Greco-Roman pagan religion simply "converted" to Christianity without changing much in the way of theology or practice. They now called themselves "Christians" but their beliefs and practices pretty much remained the same. They too had practiced sacramental and mystical religious rites with ceremonial foods, and it was easy for them to carry over the practice of their *sacramentum* and *mysterion* into the practice of the Lord's Supper.

Sacramentum originally referred to a military oath of allegiance, and then to the emblems on which the oath was taken. ... *Mysterion* was part and parcel of the stock phraseology of a host of Greek religions, and thus tended to carry the freight of its religiosity right into the life of the church. ... Religion as cult was growing right along with religion as creed in the life of the church.[1]

A third reason was theological. After the church became the dominant religion of the Roman Empire, some of the church leaders had more time to pursue theological inquiry, and one question they asked about the Lord's Supper was similar to one of the main questions about baptism. They wanted to know if grace was actually imparted to those who participated in the Lord's Supper, and if so, which elements actually imparted this grace. Since both Jesus and Paul had placed emphasis on the bread and wine, it was decided that these were the essential elements. It was theologically determined that these parts of the meal helped differentiate the "Lord's Supper" from all other meals.

But once this was decided, the next logical question was "how much" bread and wine was needed, and what kind of bread and wine? And just as with baptism, it was decided that the smallest amount would do. The amount was not what was important; it was the presence that was important. Why? Because of what Jesus said to His disciples in the upper room: "This is my body ... This is my blood."

However, as so often happens in theology, this question led to further questions. What did Jesus mean when He said, "This is

---

[1] Robert Farrar Capon, *The Astonished Heart: Reclaiming the Good News From the Lost-and-Found of Church History* (Grand Rapids: Eerdmans, 1996), 54.

my body … This is my blood?" The church leadership decided to take Jesus' words "literally" and understand that somehow, the bread and wine mystically became the body and blood of Jesus Christ. But this then led to the question of "how"? How could the bread and wine become the actual body and blood of Jesus? Again, it was decided that just as Jesus had prayed over the bread and wine before passing them around to His disciples, so also, God enabled priests to transform the bread and wine into the body and blood of Jesus through praying a special blessing upon it.

We can see that just as theological questions about baptism eventually led large portions of the church to adopt a practice of baptism by sprinkling, so also, theological inquiry about the Lord's Supper led the church to adopt a practice of giving the tiniest bits of bread and the smallest sips of juice to those who would partake of it.

It was taught that the power of the Lord's Supper was not in the full meal itself, but in the bread and wine, which, as a result of the priest's blessing, mystically transformed into the body and blood of Jesus Christ, thereby imparting grace to those who partook of it. The significance of the Lord's Supper was not in the meal itself, but in the power of the spiritual presence within the bread and wine.

Since this was so, it was not necessary for people to eat a full meal, for any amount of bread and wine would do, no matter how small. Just as baptism could be done with a few drops of water, so also the Lord's Supper could be observed with a small bit of bread and a few drops of wine.

Once "the Lord's Supper" was no longer a full meal, many

groups began to call it "communion," which is a reference to the communion of the saints with Jesus Christ. Other groups preferred to call it the "Eucharist," which means "thanksgiving." By either name, the practice does not come close to what was done by Jesus and His apostles on the night He was betrayed. The Lord's Supper had gone from a full meal in which the focus was on the community centered on Jesus Christ to a mystical religious rite in which the priestly class magically transforms normal food and drink into the actual body and blood of Jesus Christ so that those who partake of it might become one with Him.

During the Protestant Reformation, as certain church leaders began an attempt to reform the Catholic church, some Reformation leaders dropped the idea about the mystical presence of Jesus within the bread and wine, but otherwise maintained the practice as it was. The Lord's Supper continued to involve a tiny bit of bread and a few drops of wine, even though the elements were not mystically imparted with the presence of Jesus Christ. There was still some debate among the Reformers about whether the bread and wine retained a "spiritual" presence or not, but regardless of which position the various groups adopted, most groups continued to follow the tradition of eating a small bit of bread and drinking a small bit of wine.

It was in the late 19th century that some churches began to switch to grape juice, and this became the standard practice in the United Stated during Prohibition in the early 20th century. Today, some churches are starting to switch back to wine, but for the most part, the practice of the Lord's Supper as a tiny bit of bread and a small portion of grape juice (or wine) remains the same. The Lord's Supper is no longer a supper; it has become the

Savior's Snacklet or the Nazarene's Nibble.[2]

If it is surprising and challenging to think of the Lord's Supper as a full meal, think of how shocked (and hungry) an early church member would be if they attended a "Lord's Supper" as it is done today and receive nothing but a wafer of bread and teaspoon of juice. So the most surprising thing about the idea that the Lord's Supper is actually a supper is that so many Christians are surprised to learn this.

It is also somewhat ironic that Protestants criticize Catholics for too literally interpreting the word "is" in Jesus' statements "This *is* my body ... This *is* my blood" when Protestants are just as guilty for too literally interpreting the word "this" when Jesus says, "Do *this* in remembrance of me." Or maybe none of us are taking Jesus literally enough. If Jesus *literally* meant that we should do exactly what He was doing on this last night with His disciples, then we would observe the Passover meal on a yearly basis just as Jesus was doing on that night. (There are, of course, some Christians who do observe the Passover meal, but most do not.)

Instead, most Christian churches tack on "communion" at the end of a church service on a monthly or quarterly basis, in which participants reflect upon their sins, eat a wafer of tasteless bread, and drink a few drops of juice. A few people shed tears. Every time I take communion and hear the pastor quote the words of Jesus, "Do this in remembrance of me," I look around at the

[2] Bob Bryant, "Rediscovering the Lord's Supper: One Church's Journey" in *Grace in Focus* (Denton, TX: GES, 2000). Online at "Rediscovering the Lord's Supper: One Church's Journey."

bowed heads, the somber faces, and the tiny specks of bread and sips of juice held daintily in every hand, and ask myself, "Is *this* really what Jesus was telling us to do?" I think not.

But was Jesus telling us to observe the Passover meal on a regular basis? Again, I think not. Just as the word "is" in "This is my body ... This is my blood" is best understood symbolically, so also, when Jesus said, "Do this in remembrance of me," He was not saying we should literally eat the Passover meal, but should symbolically do for each other what He was doing in and through the meal for His disciples.

In the discussion above, we have seen a little bit about how the early church understood the words of Jesus and applied them to their lives. It seems that much of the trouble with the Lord's Supper came not so much from reducing it to a bit of bread and a mouthful of wine, but rather from thinking that the significance of the meal was in the bread and wine themselves. Even today, churches that do not believe anything mystical happens to the bread and wine still believe that the bread and wine (or juice) themselves are what is important, and that this "meal" must be observed on a set schedule.

Furthermore, many believers who are involved in distributing the bread and juice in their church might have experienced the strange "discussion" with a deacon, elder, or pastor after a communion service about what to do with the leftover bread and juice. You will often be severely rebuked if you suggest throwing the bread out or dumping the juice down the drain. One does not treat the "body and blood of Jesus" in such a profane way! So it seems that even in churches that practice a "purely symbolic" form of the Lord's Supper, the bread and juice are still viewed as holy and sacred elements.

In all these ways, the true significance and importance of the Lord's Supper has all but vanished and we are left with little more than a dead and empty religious and mystical rite. In reality, our modern rite more closely resembles the heretical Gnostic mystery rites than the community meal instituted by Jesus. In his penetrating book, *Against the Protestant Gnostics,* Philip J. Lee sounds this alarm:

> [The Lord's Supper] has been spiritualized to the extent that it could scarcely be recognized as a meal at all. The purely symbolic wafer of the Roman celebration … has in most Protestant churches been replaced by minute, carefully diced pieces of bread unlike any other bread ever eaten by any culture. The common cup which the medieval Church withheld from the faithful is, except among Anglicans, still the sole possession of the clergy. The unordained are now given thimble-like glasses filled with Welch's grape juice. The symbolism is quite clear. We all come before God individually; with our individual bits of bread and our individual cups of juice, we are not of one loaf and one chalice. Our relationship to Christ is private and personal. What may be even more significant is that by partaking of this unearthly meal with our unbreadly bread and our unwinely wine we are making a clear statement that the bread and wine of spiritual communion has no connection with earthly communion. It is an unmistakable gnostic witness against the significance of ordinary meals: common bread, wine, the table fellowship of laughter and tears.
>
> … Concreteness, the preciseness of home-baked bread and earthy red wine, in pottery, plates and chalices, received with much chewing and swallowing, witnesses to the mystery of the Word made

flesh. The present practice unwittingly undercuts the mystery and leaves us with the vague and unhelpful feeling that some undefined perfunctory act must be taking place.[3]

Maybe it is time to crucify and bury the Lord's Supper so that it can rise again to new meaning and significance in the church today. Maybe it is time to truly return to the instructions of Jesus so that we can "Do *this* in remembrance of me."

THE LORD'S SUPPER TODAY

Observing the Lord's Supper today must begin with understanding what exactly it is we are observing. We have hinted at this above, and will see it in more detail below, but no one says it better than Robert Farrar Capon:

> Consider the scene in church on a Sunday. Here are a bunch of people, more or less dressed to the nines, in an expensive building, with maybe very spectacular music and even a paid choir, *deliberately celebrating the worst thing the human race—which includes them— has ever done; the murder of God Incarnate.*[4]

The closest equivalent might be like celebrating the holocaust. Who would do such a thing? And yet in a sense, Christians celebrate the murder of God every time they take communion.

Capon may have overstated his case somewhat. Christians are

---

[3] Philip J. Lee, *Against the Protestant Gnostics* (New York: Oxford, 1987), 272-273.

[4] Robert Farrar Capon, *The Mystery of Christ... & Why We Don't Get It* (Grand Rapids: Eerdmans, 1993), 127. Italics his.

not so much celebrating what *they have done* to Jesus, but rather, what *He has done* for us. We are not celebrating that we killed Him. Far from it. We are celebrating that He came, and died, and most importantly of all, rose again from the dead, so that through Him, the entire world is forgiven of all their sin and eternal life is freely given to those who believe in Jesus for it. We are celebrating that, in Jesus, a new community of God has been birthed upon the earth, a new Exodus is happening to all creation, and freedom and liberty has been proclaimed to all who were enslaved to sin, death, and the devil. When we observe the Lord's Supper, this is what we celebrate.

So one has to wonder if a five-minute ceremony with a tiny cracker and shot-glass of wine is a proper celebration. It seems that something much grander, much more enjoyable, much more celebratory, is needed. We need something where the food and drink flow freely. Where there is laughter and smiles, where life is enjoyed to the full.

Maybe the best way to observe the Lord's Supper is to follow the example of the church and celebrate it around food. Lots of food. And drink. Lots of drink. Enough drink that there is some danger of people getting drunk (1 Cor 11:21). There is something sacred about gathering with other people around food and drink, and it often seems that more fellowship and relationship development can occur during one two-hour feast, than over an entire year of Sunday church services. Maybe a good replacement for the Sunday service would be a weekly or monthly feast.

In fact, if people are part of a traditional church, I would encourage them to find a group of people with whom they can regularly eat. And while there does not have to be a time of formal teaching or sharing in such a meal, it might be good to pause during the meal and remember the sacrifice that Jesus made in His body and by His blood for all people. This time does not necessarily need to be subdued and gloomy, but can be a time of rejoicing. Remembering Jesus as part of a meal could be more like saying a toast, for Jesus is why we eat; Jesus is why we laugh; Jesus is why we live; Jesus is why we love.

Having said this, however, it is important that we avoid the mistakes of the past and do not simply trade one traditional ritual for another. I am not saying what "should" be done; only what "could" be done. If all we do is trade a bit of bread and wine for a full meal, but retain our view of the meal as a mystical rite, or retain the legalistic requirement of the meal as part of what "true" Christians do on a regular basis, then we have missed the entire point of what Jesus was saying in that Last Supper with His disciples.

It is time for the church to step back from the ritualistic aspects of the Lord's Supper, and especially to step back from the mystical, magical, and legalistic elements that have crept into this ceremony, and reconsider once again what exactly it was that Jesus was doing and saying when He said, "This is my body ... This is my blood ... Do this in remembrance of me." He was not primarily referring to the bread. He was not primarily referring to the wine. He was not even primarily referring to the meal. Instead, it is the other things Jesus said in this meal which help us understand what Jesus was doing. Once we understand this, we can then understand how to observe the "Lord's Supper" today.

In the Last Supper, when Jesus gathered His disciples around the table in the upper room to share the Passover meal, He pointed the elements of the Passover meal to Himself. I have no intention of going through each element of the Jewish Passover meal to show how the various items on the table and the various cups of wine symbolically represent the message and ministry of Jesus Christ, for this is not what is important for our purposes here.[5] What is important is the big picture significance of what Jesus was doing with the meal, and then also what He specifically said regarding the significance of the bread and the wine.

First of all, the meal is significant in itself because of what it represents. By pointing the Passover meal to Himself, Jesus taught His disciples the principle of redemption. The meal is intended to show how Jesus redeems all things. As pointed out in this chapter, Christians today often overlook the fact that the Last Supper was actually a Passover meal. But even among those who recognize that Jesus and His disciples were observing the Passover, the true significance of what Jesus was doing is often missed.

Christians who understand that Jesus was observing the Passover sometimes think that through these actions, Jesus was endorsing the Passover as something that should be observed by all future followers of Jesus. But a cursory glance through the Book of Acts and the New Testament epistles indicates that the early church did not understand Jesus to be teaching this at all, for there is no call anywhere for Gentile believers to adopt the practice of observing the Passover.

Instead, what we see is that some Gentile believers continued

---

[5] If this sort of study interests you, there are numerous books on the subject. See, for example, Ceil & Moishe Rosen, *Christ in the Passover* (Chicago: Moody, 1978).

THE RITE OF COMMUNION 99

to practice some of their own celebrations and festive meals, but reinterpreted in light of Jesus Christ. We see this here and there throughout the Book of Acts, but it is especially bought out in some of the letters of Paul, where he writes about the practice of some Colossians in observing their festivals and new moon celebrations (Col 2:16). It is also likely that this continued practice is behind the Corinthians controversy about eating meat sacrificed to idols (1 Cor 8:4-9). In these ways, we see that the early church properly understood what Jesus was teaching.

When Jesus said, "Do this in remembrance of me," He wasn't saying, "Eat the Passover meal." No, He was saying, "Practice redemption as I have done here." Jesus was Jewish and so He filled the Jewish festivals, celebrations, and holidays with new meaning and significance. He centered these holidays around Himself. He redeemed the Jewish holidays by pointing them to Himself, just as He had redeemed the Hebrew Scriptures, the Temple Mount, the Priestly class, and everything else related to Judaism. In so doing, Jesus was not saying "Judaism is right and everybody else is wrong," but rather, "I am the way, the truth, and the life, and everything else can be reinterpreted and repurposed to point to Me."

Just as Jesus redeemed people by transferring us out of the kingdom of darkness and into the kingdom of light so that where we used to point others to sin, death, and the devil, we now point people to grace, life, and Jesus Christ, so also, Jesus did this with Judaism, and instructed His followers (that's us) to do the same thing with our customs, cultures, traditions, and yes, even religions. Jesus is in the business of redemption, and when He pointed the Passover meal to Himself and said "Do this in remembrance of me," He was inviting all who would follow Him to do as He has done in redeeming and reconciling all things to Himself, so that ultimately, God may be all in all (1 Cor 15:28).

So the first purpose of what Jesus did during this Last Supper was to teach His disciples the big-picture principle of redemption. But then, by pointing specifically to the bread and the wine, Jesus went on to show two additional purposes for this meal, which again are often missed by Christians today.

When Jesus took up the bread, and broke it, He said, "This is My body which is broken for you; do this in remembrance of me" (1 Cor 11:24). Far too often, Christians get all caught up in what the word "is" means, or symbolism of the unleavened bread as Christ's sinless body. What we often fail to emphasize is what Jesus Himself emphasized, namely, the brokenness. When Jesus said, "Do this ..." He was not instructing His disciples to eat unleavened bread or to somehow mystically transform the bread into His body. No, Jesus was telling His disciples to live lives of brokenness, just as He had done.

To live a life of brokenness is to live life for others. To live so that you think of others more than you think of yourself. To sacrifice your goals, your dreams, your riches, your time, your desires, and your energy for the sake of others.

To live a life of brokenness is also to live life with the recognition that because of sin, we *are* broken. Sometimes pastors give the impression that by using unleavened bread, Jesus was indicating that just as He was sinless, so also, we must live sinless lives. I think Jesus was saying the opposite. He was calling us to recognize our sinfulness and live in light of it. Because of sin, we *are* broken, which means that none of us have all the answers, all the truth, or all that is needed to live in wholeness. We need each other. Because of our sin and our brokenness, Jesus calls us to walk in honesty and humility, recognizing that only in community is there wholeness and life.

So in pointing the broken bread to Himself and then instructing His disciples to "Do this in remembrance of me," Jesus was not primarily telling His followers to eat the unleavened bread of the Passover, but was telling them to follow His example in living in brokenness with other people. This is what Jesus did in His earthly ministry, and what God has been doing for all humanity since we first sinned in the Garden of Eden.

Finally, when Jesus took up the cup of wine after supper, He said, "This cup is the new covenant in my blood. This do, as often as you drink it, in remembrance of me" (1 Cor 11:25). Just as with the bread, many Christians focus on the word "is" or the wine itself. But Jesus is not focused on the wine, or what happens to it (if anything). Instead, He talks about the "New Covenant." In this part of the Lord's Supper, Jesus was not telling His followers to drink the wine, but to drink regularly and freely from the New Covenant.

What is this Covenant? It is the covenant that replaces the Old Covenant. It is a new agreement, and new "Last Will and Testament," a new way of doing things, and new contract.[6] It is a covenant of love. Of community, forgiveness, grace, reconciliation, equality, friendship, joy, celebration, and freedom. The New

---

[6] See Maxine Armstrong, *The 1 Commandment* (Dallas, OR: Redeeming Press, 2014).

Covenant is what Jesus talked about when He began His earthly ministry (Luke 4:18-19), and what Jesus exemplified through everything He did and said during His earthly ministry.

In pointing the cup of wine to Himself and then instructing His disciples to "Do this in remembrance of me," Jesus was not primarily telling His followers to drink the last cup of wine of the Passover meal, but was telling them to live in light of the New Covenant, which He had revealed to the world through His life, words, and actions.

So when Jesus says, "This is my body … This is my blood … Do this in remembrance of me," He is not primarily referring to the bread, the wine, or even to the meal. No, He is referring to what He has just taught. He is inviting His disciples—and therefore us as well—to live as a new covenant community, full of redemption, brokenness, and grace. He is calling us to treat others as we wish to be treated. To freely forgive as we have been forgiven. To treat others as equals, with dignity and respect. To celebrate, laugh, and rejoice in the freedom we have in Christ.

When Jesus says, "Do this in remembrance of me," we could understand Him to be saying, "Do this in imitation of me." Imitate what? His life! A true "Lord's Supper" is not a bit of bread and drink of wine tacked on to the end of a Sunday church service, but is rather a life that is lived in light of Jesus Christ. The true Lord's Supper is a life that looks like Jesus. It is a life that lives in constant remembrance and imitation of Him.

CONCLUSION

Do you want to observe the Lord's Supper today as it has traditionally been done for about 1500 years? Go ahead! If you want participate in "communion" or the "Eucharist," it is not wrong. But just remember that the true "Lord's Supper" is about living lives of redemption, brokenness, and grace with others.

How can you do this? You are only limited by your creativity and imagination.

First, seek to redeem. Find customs, celebrations, or places that can be repurposed and reconfigured so that where they used to turn people away from God, they now point people to Jesus Christ.

Second, recognize your own brokenness, and seek to live broken before others. Look around your neighborhood for people you can serve. Find someone to sacrificially love. Go mow their lawn. Bring them meals after their surgery. Help them fix the roof on their garage. Watch their kids for free.

Third, live in light of the New Covenant. Live life to the full. Be extravagant and lavish with grace, love, and forgiveness. Have a party. Invite lots of people over. Put out the best food and serve it on the best dishes. Laugh. Tell jokes. Sing and dance, if that's your thing. Just enjoy life with other people. Pour out your life for the reconciliation and deliverance of others. Forgive when it is not deserved. Love when it is not earned. Show mercy. Be gracious. Laugh. Rejoice. In a word: live. Truly live.

The Lord's Supper is not about bread and wine. It is not even about a meal. Though these sorts of things can symbolize what Jesus taught on that last night with His disciples, the true Lord's Supper is a life lived in light of Jesus Christ. Jesus lived His life as He did so that we might imitate Him. Do you want to observer the Lord's Supper? Live as He lived, in remembrance of Him.

DISCUSSION QUESTIONS

1. Why is communion special or important to you? What about this ceremony makes it special?

2. What was the event which Jesus observed with His disciples at the first "Lord's Supper?" Does this shed any light on the words of Jesus when He says, "As often as you *eat this bread*, and *drink this cup*, do it in remembrance of me" (1 Cor 11:26)?

3. In Acts and 1 Corinthians, how are the early Christians observing the Lord's Supper?

4. How did the early church transition from a yearly observance of Passover to a daily or weekly time of food and fellowship? What are some of the factors that led to this transition?

5. How did the church go from observing the Lord's Supper around a meal with lots of laughter, food, and drink, to eating a little cracker with a thumbnail of grape juice?

6. What is the true significance of the Lord's Supper? What major point was Jesus showing His disciples?

7. When Jesus says, "Do *this* in remembrance of me," what was He *really* talking about? Was it just the meal? Or was it the true significance of the meal?

8. If we do not partake of "communion," is this wrong? Are there other (more significant) ways they can remember and imitate what Jesus revealed at the Last Supper?

PART II:
GIVE UP YOUR RIGHTS

*The real truth is that there is something about human
nature which makes it capable of being inspired by
what it believes to be right to do both wonderful and
appalling things.*
—*Ravi Zacharias*

I wrote this paragraph on March 23, 2012. It was the 237th anniversary of the day Patrick Henry spoke these immortal words:

Is life so dear, or peace so sweet, as to be purchased at the price of chains and slavery? Forbid it, Almighty God! I know not what course others may take; but as for me, give me liberty, or give me death!

Upon hearing this, the crowd reportedly rose to their feet and shouted, "To arms! To arms!"

I love this quote from one of our nation's founding fathers, as I love much of the history and values of our great country. But I am often surprised and perplexed that men who wrote in the

Declaration of Independence that all men are created equal and are endowed by their Creator with the unalienable rights of life, liberty, and the pursuit of happiness, could so quickly seek to take the first of those rights—the right of life—from others.

In other words, it is a strange world indeed that seeks to defend liberty and the right to life by taking away the liberty and the right to life of others.

I understand that this is the way the world works, and that these calls to war are in the interest of national self-defense, but I also understand that the way of the world rarely matches the way of Jesus, and that usually, both sides of a particular battle or war are able to justify their actions as "self-defense." Even aggressors like the Nazis and Al-Qaeda say that what they are doing is for the strengthening and preservation of their culture, society, and economy.

So while it is true that all people are created equal, and that God has given us the right to life, liberty, and the pursuit of happiness, it is not true that the best way to achieve these rights is through the subjection, enslavement, and killing of others. For do not others also have the unalienable right to life, liberty, and the pursuit of happiness?

But what happens when rights collide? What happens when one person's pursuit of happiness requires the unhappiness of someone else, or worse, their enslavement and death?

It is here that the way of Jesus is highly instructive. It is also here where the founding fathers of our government, as well as nearly all governments of the world, have missed the mark. And it is also here where most Christians, pastors, and churches have lost the way of Jesus. For these reasons, Section 2 of this book chalus is best lived, not by

om them for the sake of

and the pursuit of hap-

n offered to Jesus were

biness are good. God is

Such things are divine

ns. They are not, how-

d in Scripture, and are

are divorced from the

d for how we live our

reatest instruments of

has ever seen. When

our rights become sa-

western society and

al. "We are dominat-

that rule American

eedom of choice, dis-

personal freedoms,

t of others. Individu-

vn life full of happi-

e lives of others, be-

nopes and dreams of

iberty, and the pur-

Harper Collins, 1998),

lenges Christians to follow Jesus by giving up their rights. As we will see, Jesus, in contrast to Patrick Henry, said, "I give you liberty *by* my death!" Christians and churches should follow this example as we seek to be Jesus in the world.

Please note that the following two chapters should not be seen as an attack on the United States, the Declaration of Independence, or the Constitution. I love this country and I love the ideas expressed in our founding documents. I am proud to be a citizen of the United States of America. I love the fact that I live and work here, and that my children can grow up in what is arguably one of the best countries in the world. I love what our nation stands for, and I love much of our nation's history. Sure, there are some things in our history that grieve me, and there are numerous activities the United States is currently involved in that I would like to see changed. But in general, I think the United States has a noble history of trying to do what is right and best in and for the world. We often get things wrong, but there is much that is praiseworthy and honorable.

However, it sometimes seems that the values expressed by our government as found within the Declaration of Independence and Constitutional Bill of Rights, conflict with the values of Jesus and the Kingdom of Heaven as found within the pages of Scripture. As Christians become aware of these conflicts, we are forced to choose between them. We must try to follow the example of Peter who chose to please God rather than men (Acts 5:29), and the example of Paul (who was himself a citizen of Rome) that above all else, we are citizens of heaven (Php 3:20). Our true loyalties must not lie with any worldly government or geographical location, but with Jesus Christ and the rule and reign of God on earth.

Yet though nearly all Christians and churches pa
to living as citizens of the Kingdom of Heaven and p
rather than men, our actual behavior betrays where (
lie. I fear that more and more, churches sacrifice the g(
altar of Constitutional rights. This is usually not inte.
is based on an attempt to defend and protect Christi
know it. We believe it is essential for the church to
building on Sunday morning, and are quick to sue a
ment official who seems to block or restrict our right t
We feel that we should be able to say whatever we wai
pulpit and in our church publications—no matter ho
it might be to others—because we have the freedom of

Even many sermons and Sunday school programs f(
themes of our right to life, liberty, and the pursuit of
which are not exactly found in Scripture but instead ai
of the European Enlightenment. It was Thomas Hobb
thor of *Leviathan* (1651), who taught that since everyb(
life, liberty, and happiness, these goals must therefore b
to our nature. To deny them would be to deny our "C
nature as humans. There are numerous problems wit
idea, not least among them that Scripture and the exan
sus seem to disagree. Nevertheless, it is not uncommc
sermons about how to live our best life now, how tc
freedom and liberty, and how to have a happy life, ha
happy kids, and a happy job.

In these calls for life, liberty, and the pursuit of I
where are the gospel themes of self-sacrifice, service, hu
and death? They are utterly and totally absent. In sermo

(Luke 4:1-13). Maybe the gospel of Je
fighting for our "rights" but by fleeing f
others.

This does not mean that life, liberty
piness are bad. No. The things that Sa
good things, just as life, liberty, and ha
on the side of life, liberty, and happines
gifts and should be possessed by all hun
ever, God-given "rights," are not guaran
not worth killing for. When our "right
understanding that we will answer to C
lives, these rights become some of the
death, enslavement, and sadness the wc
separated from subservience to the gosp
tanic. This is what we see all around us.

In many ways, these rights have ca
culture to become self-centered and ego
ed by the essentially Enlightenment v.
culture: pursuit of happiness, unrestrict(
dain for authority."[1] People demand
even if it causes the bondage and enslave
als do everything necessary to make the
ness and joy, even if it means destroyii
traying friends and family, and ruining
countless people. When some run after

[1] Dallas Willard, *The Divine Conspiracy* (Ne
214.

suit of happiness, they seek the power to do as they please with little or no thought about the life, liberty, or happiness of others. Sometimes, when we stand on our right to assemble, or to say whatever we want, we often do so without regard for how our actions and words might inconvenience, offend, or psychologically wound others.

Far too often, churches fall into the same trap. In the next two chapters, we will look at seven rights frequently claimed by Christians and churches. Three are from the Declaration of Independence: the rights to life, liberty, and the pursuit of happiness. The final four are from the Bill of Rights in the Constitution: the right to practice religion, the right to free speech, the right to assemble, and the right to bear arms. In each section, we will look at the value of these rights from a humanitarian perspective, and then how the right can be misused and abused when divorced from God and the gospel, and how churches are guilty of this as well. Each section will conclude with what Scripture teaches about this right, and how it could be lived out within the liberating confines of the gospel.

As we will see, the gospel calls us to give up our rights as we follow Jesus into the world.

DISCUSSION QUESTIONS

1. When do our "rights" become wrong to pursue?

2. Do you feel that pastors should have the right to say anything they want from the pulpit, regardless of who it might hurt?

CHAPTER 3

CERTAIN UNALIENABLE RIGHTS

The founding fathers of the United States of America wrote in the Declaration of Independence that all men are endowed by the creator with certain unalienable rights, and among these are life, liberty, and the pursuit of happiness. They also stated that the truthfulness of these rights were "self-evident." I have sometimes wondered how "self-evident" the truth of these rights really are since it seems that most governments, rulers, and authorities throughout world history have been blind to these rights, but that is a philosophical question best reserved for another time.

The question that concerns us now is not so much about whether or not these rights are self-evident, or even whether or not they are truly divinely-ordained rights. Assuming that these truths are self-evident, and assuming that they are endowed by God upon all people, the question we must answer is how we are to go about obtaining, protecting, and defending these rights in a world that seems so intent on destroying them. *Can* such rights be won by war, and if so, *should* they be? Are the rights to life, liberty, and the pursuit of happiness worth fighting for?

At first, such questions seem almost rhetorical. If God has given certain unalienable rights to all people, and there are some who seek to deny these rights to others, is it not our responsibility to defend our God-given rights by defeating those who would take them away? It seems like the answer is obvious. And yet, a moment's reflection often causes a small check in the back of our minds about what we are doing when we go to war against others in the defense of our freedoms. A bigger check in the back of our minds occurs when we hear our so-called enemies saying the same things in defense of their actions as we say in defense of ours. How can we be certain we are "in the right" when we attack others in defense of our liberties when they claim to only be defending theirs?

The difficulties of such questions are more easily seen when we reword the questions: Can the rights to life, liberty, and the pursuit of happiness be won by taking away these same rights from others through war? Even if we could gain such rights for ourselves through battle and bloodshed, is this the "right" thing to do? Does the universal rights of all people to life, liberty, and the pursuit of happiness preclude our desire to fight for these rights against those who would deny them to us?

These are harder questions, aren't they? And as is the nature with questions, asking hard questions rarely leads to answers, but only to more questions: Could it be possible that while life, liberty, and the pursuit of happiness are unalienable rights given equally by God to all, we can only die for these rights by dying to them? Could it be possible that Jesus Himself showed us how to gain these rights for the world, and His example revealed that life, liberty, and the pursuit of happiness cannot be obtained for ourselves, but can only be obtained for others *by dying to them* ourselves? Might it not be true that as Jesus suffered, bled, and died on the cross, He not only gained life, liberty, and happiness for others, but also showed the way for all who would follow Him how we too could fight for the rights of others? What if, when the chief priests and scribes mocked Jesus as He hung on the cross by saying, "He saved others, but He cannot save Himself," they were actually stating the foundational and fundamental law of God's universe?[1] What if the "deeper magic" of creation is not that we win only by killing, but that we can never win unless we die, and only by our dying can others win?

In the following pages we will look at the "certain unalienable right" of life, liberty, and the pursuit of happiness and see that, if Jesus is our guide, we gain these rights for ourselves and others only by dying to them. Death always precedes resurrection, and if we refuse to die, we will never experience life, liberty, or happiness. It is only by dying to our rights that we fight for them.

RIGHT TO LIFE

No one can deny that all people desire and deserve life. It is for life that God created this world, and it is through life that we glorify God. Even those who live without God know that all people deserve life, which is why the penalty of death is reserved for our worst criminals. And murder, which is wrongfully taking the life of another, is viewed by all cultures as one of the worst crimes that can be committed. So it is natural and normal to claim our right to life.

---

[1] C. S. Lewis, *Yours, Jack: Spiritual Direction from C. S. Lewis* (New York: HarperCollins, 2008), 138.

Problems arise, however, when, in our attempts to maintain and preserve our life, we fail to recognize the source of all life, namely God, and that because all life derives from Him, every other person on this earth has just as much of a right to life as we. Divorced from God, an individual's right to life can lead them to kill and destroy the lives of the innocent, the weak, the poor, the voiceless, and defenseless. Thousands of people are killed through genocide or war when one group of people decides that the way they want to live their life requires the death of others.

There are numerous examples of this throughout history and in modern practice. We have all heard of tragic events where one person murders another out of greed, jealousy, fits of rage, or selfish ambition. We could point out modern warfare and how all war robs others of life in the attempt to keep the right to life for ourselves. But these sorts of examples are the obvious ones. There are others which are far less obvious.

Take, for example, the practice of sacrificing of our children in the name of business and success. We don't do that! Or do we? In ancient Canaanite culture, some people literally sacrificed their children by laying their infant babies in the hands of the god Molech, under which a raging fire had been ignited until the hands glowed red-hot. The infants were literally fried to death. This was done in the belief that Molech would give the parents prosperity in their business, crops in their fields, and success in life.

Despite the modern-day assumption that we have made progress from such barbaric horrors, our only real progress is in our ability to hide, mask, and rename the same exact horrors that go on in our culture. Today, we sacrifice our children through abortion and neglect as we strive after success in business and the next big promotion. Just like Molech worshippers of previous genera-tions, we kill and neglect our children because they get in the way of our plans and goals.

Do not children also have a right to life? Where are the fathers and mothers who will lay down their hopes, dreams, and career goals for the sake of their children? Where are the parents who will get by on a smaller budget so that one parent can stay home and raise the children? Why do husband and wives so easily get divorced, knowing that such a separation will cause long-term psychological and emotional devastation in the lives of their chil-dren? It is not enough for Christian parents to believe in the "right to life" if they don't also believe that once the life of a child is brought into this world, they still have that same "right to life" to become all that God wants for each and every child.

We can move on to other groups of people as well. While some churches do speak against abortion, we usually also con-demn the single mothers or young couples who feel that abortion is the only way out of a difficult situation. It is so much easier to condemn the mother for aborting her pregnancy, when in reality, churches are often guilty of setting up such conditions in which the mother feels she has no choice but to abort. When a young woman gets pregnant out of wedlock, rather than come around her in love and support, with promises to protect and provide, we more often than not cast her out like a sheep among wolves. In refusing to provide help to the woman who is considering an abortion, we are not only complicit in the death of her child when she gets an abortion, but also in the ongoing devastation of her own life as well.

The same exact logic can be applied to drunkards, drug addicts, and prostitutes. It is easy to condemn them from our cushioned pews and Bible studies, but such condemnation is nothing more than a death-sentence we pass down when we care more for our life of ease and comfort than the life of those deemed less worthy of it.

Take the LGBT community as an example. Though the tide is changing, there are still many churches and Christians that condemn and shun those who are lesbian, gay, bisexual, or transgender. In many ways, LGBT people get turned away from our churches more than murderers and rapists. Whatever your convictions are about lesbians, gays, bisexuals, and transgenders, shouldn't they be loved and accepted just like anyone else? Even if you think that their lifestyle is "sinful," why would a church choose to condemn and reject LGBT people, while at the same time love and accept people who are guilty of other sins? Does not the Bible speak more against gluttony, greed, anger, pride, and violence than homosexuality? Why then does the church focus on homosexuality, while ignoring the sins for which we are almost all universally guilty and which the Bible speaks against much more frequently?

I am sorry if this sounds like a blanket condemnation of the church. It is not. Thankfully, there have always been numerous churches in various cities and towns that show grace, love, and acceptance to others. Maybe your church is one of these.

Yet there is still a wide gap between the typical church and whole segments of society which we would rather judge, condemn, and ignore than love, accept, and serve. By our actions and our words, we tell these people groups that they do not have the right to life, and the world would be better off if they just died.

What people groups are these? Some are people of other religions we have trouble accepting, like Muslims, for example. We often view Muslims as the enemy and as a challenge to our faith. We sometimes condemn Islam as a violent religion, while forgetting that much violence through the centuries (and even in recent decades) has been done in the name of Jesus Christ. Christians are often just as guilty about calling for the death of our enemies as Muslims are in calling for the death of theirs. We accuse Muslims of teaching a "Convert or die" message, but Christians often have their own version of this message.

We may not (usually) kill people who refuse to convert, but there are numerous examples of Christians gleefully telling non-Christians that if they do not convert, they will suffer and burn eternally in hell. Does not "Turn or burn" sound very much like "Convert of die"? I am not a Universalist, but this "turn or burn" message is not found in Scripture, nor does it come from the mouth of Jesus.[2] To the contrary, when some of Jesus' disciples asked if they could call down fire from heaven upon a town because the people did not accept Jesus, He rebuked His disciples for even thinking such a thing (Luke 9:54-56). Could it really be true that the same Jesus who refused to burn a town to the ground because they did not believe in Him, would then turn around and burn these people forever in hell?

---

[2] Some people claim that Jesus teaches more about hell than He does about heaven. They point to His teachings about fire, Gehenna, and the passages on the "weeping and gnashing of teeth" as proof. I am convinced that few (if any) of these passages actually describe a place of eternal, conscious torment. Some of these Scriptures might actually describe one particular aspect of heaven. See my book, *Am I Going to Hell?* (Dallas, OR: Redeeming Press, 2019).

Even when we are able to graciously love certain sinners like addicts and prostitutes, or become friends with people of other religions, there are still some groups of people which receive almost universal hatred. Like who? Human traffickers, rapists, and child molesters. These certainly are some of the worst crimes that a human can commit, and those who do them should be sent to prison. But is this the same thing as calling for their death? Or, if they are released from prison, does not the grace of God in our lives call upon us to somehow seek their restoration and reintegration into society? But how can this happen if churches and Christians continue to condemn, reject, and shun them? I understand that we must protect our children at all costs, but is there no way for churches to show love and forgiveness to former child molesters while protecting our children at the same time? With some Spirit-inspired creative thinking, there must be, for, lest we forget it, Jesus also died for child molesters. I wonder if the church could find a way to die for them as well?

If the church is going to follow the example of Jesus in giving up His life for us, we can begin by discerning who it is we would die for, and then seek to sacrifice our life for them instead. It is not a matter of saying that sin doesn't matter. It does. But the problem of sin is not solved by condemning it and shunning those who commit it. The power of sin is defeated by entering in to the life of the sinner, and walking through life with them. It will be painful and messy, but this is the only way to give our life for the lives of others.

The church, for the sake of our witness, must regain the courage to nonviolently venture out in faith into dens of lions, fiery furnaces, and up to the hills on which we will be crucified.[3]

Such an idea is not new to the church. The church has been practicing self-sacrificial love and forgiveness since the beginning. The problem is that we have become selective about who receives our love. If we are going to die to ourselves, if we are going to love as Jesus loved, if we are going to seek the "right to life" for others, then we must give the love, grace, and mercy to all other people that we want them to show to us. This statement by Greg Boyd should be plastered on the pulpit of every church in America:

> Evangelical churches are usually refuge houses for *certain kinds* of sinners—the loveless, the self-righteous, those apathetic toward the poor and unconcerned with issues of justice and race, the greedy, the gluttons, and so on. People guilty of *those* sins usually feel little discomfort among us. But evangelical churches are not usually safe places for other kinds of sinners—those whose sins, ironically, tend to be much less frequently mentioned in the Bible than the religiously sanctioned sins.

> It is rare indeed that a drunkard, drug addict, or prostitute would think of going to church because he or she just needed to feel loved and accepted. These people may go to bars, fellow addicts, drug dealers, or pimps to find refuge and acceptance, but they would not

---

[3] Tripp York and Justin Barringer, eds., *A Faith Not Worth Fighting For* (Eugene, OR: Wipf & Stock, 2012), 103.

go to church.[4]

This sort of attitude is nothing short of hypocritical. By classifying some sins as less forgivable than others, or some people as less worthy of our love and acceptance, we have forsaken the gospel and abandoned the message of life in Jesus Christ, and have replaced it with our own unloving, judgmental condemnation of others. By our words and our actions, we tell others that we have no place for them in our life.

Loving others and fellowship with them does not mean that we condone a particular way of living. This is true whether we are talking about the sin of child molestation or gluttony, murder or gossip. Why is it that we can love and forgive some types of sin, but not others? When we condemn others, we are essentially condemning them to death, which is something Jesus did not do, and as His followers, nor should we.

One key to helping us live this way, is to remember that our struggle is not against flesh and blood, but against spiritual forces of wickedness (Eph 6:10-20). One primary goal of the principalities and powers is to block the work of God in this life. And as God's task is to bring the unalienable right to life for all people, the spiritual forces arrayed against God love nothing more than when we humans hate and kill one another. If God is for life, then His enemies are for death. And if we use the right to life as

---

[4] Gregory A. Boyd, *Repenting of Religion: Turning from Judgment to the Love of God* (Grand Rapids: Baker, 2004), 103. Regarding the issue of the church's attitude toward lesbians, gays, bisexuals, and transgenders, see Andrew Marin, *Love in an Orientation: Elevating the Conversation with the Gay Community* (Downer's Grove: IVP, 2009).

justification for the killing of others, God's enemies have succeed-
ed, not only in taking life, but in twisting and perverting the right
to life into something it was never meant to be. When our personal right to life is used as a right to kill others, the right to life is
twisted and perverted so that it no longer serves God, but serves
our enemy, the devil.

The right to life can only be used when it is used for the sake
of others. Like Jesus, we must give up our lives for others, even
for our enemies, so that through our death, they might have a
chance at life.

Will accepting, loving, and forgiving certain types of people
make us uncomfortable, make church life difficult and possibly
even dangerous, and ruin the sense of peace and security we feel
in a Sunday morning service? It might. But that's okay, because
that is what the gospel is about. The gospel is not about living our
life the way we want. There is no right to life written in the gospel, unless it is the right to eternal life, which is promised to all
people, regardless of what they have done. The gospel of Jesus
Christ is about life and forgiveness for all people, no matter what.

Following Jesus, we're called to manifest the beauty of an outra-
geously impractical life that would sooner be killed than kill.

So, while we can affirm the right to life as a noble political value, as
Kingdom people we have to revolt against the temptation to this
noble value above the value of self-sacrificial love in order to mani-

fest the beauty of the Jesus-looking Kingdom.[5]

RIGHT TO LIBERTY

Liberty is one of the most valued and cherished possessions in the entire world. People who face tyranny and enslavement, or suffer under harsh and cruel governments, long for liberty and freedom. People who have never tasted freedom will give up almost anything to obtain it, and those who have lost their liberty, dream day and night of regaining it once again.

It is for these reasons, and many others, that the Declaration of Independence lists liberty as one of the unalienable rights of all people. All people deserve to be free people, based simply on the fact that they are people. The basis for the liberty of all is further enforced when the Scriptures are considered. God, as the ultimate free being, made mankind in His image, and as such we also long to be free. So it is no surprise that the theme of freedom is found everywhere in Scripture. It is not an exaggeration to say that deliverance from bondage and slavery is one of the primary themes in all of Scripture. And while slavery did exist in the days of Jesus and the apostles, biblical authors like Paul taught that slaves should be treated with dignity and respect as children of God, and even be given freedom (see Philemon; Eph 6:9). This New Testament attitude toward slavery has its foundation in the Old Testament Scriptures.

---

[5] Gregory A. Boyd, *The Myth of a Christian Religion* (Grand Rapids: Zondervan, 2009), 84-85.

One of the greatest and most foundational stories in Scripture is the deliverance of Israel from slavery in Egypt. While under bondage, they cried out for deliverance, and God sent them Moses to rescue them from slavery and lead them to liberty and freedom in the Promised Land. The rest of Scripture reveals the repetitive cycle between liberty and bondage that the Israelites experienced, so that by the time John the Baptist and Jesus of Nazareth began their ministries, the Hebrew people were once again in a state of bondage to a foreign power, this time to the Roman Empire.

The rest of the New Testament also shows that while Jesus did not come to free Israel from Roman occupation, He was focused on liberating the world from bondage to sin, death, and Satan. His entire ministry was for the purpose of liberating the captives and releasing those who were enslaved (Luke 4:18-29). The desire for freedom and liberation are not only built into the heart and soul of every person on earth, but seem to be confirmed and supported as a good and godly desire within the pages of Scripture. As such, Thomas Jefferson was right to list liberty as one of our certain unalienable rights.

Yet just as with any desire or longing, when liberty is divorced from God, it can become a great danger and even an idol. No true liberty can exist apart from submission to God. Liberty apart from service to God is nothing more than bondage. This can be seen in various ways.

First, liberty becomes bondage when we seek liberty above God. I recently heard a conservative radio talk-show host say that mankind's greatest desire is liberty. Though I would agree that all people long for liberty, I would not say that it is the greatest desire of all.[6] As soon as we begin to place our desire for liberty above our desire for God, the goal of liberty becomes our master. We become slaves of liberty. And liberty, as a goal and cause in itself, becomes a terrible taskmaster, sending people to their death and exacting horrific crimes on people and nations which are viewed as obstructing our liberty. The quest for liberty and freedom has even backfired on ourselves.

> What we got was not self-freedom but self-centeredness, loneliness, superficiality, and harried consumerism. Free is not how many of our citizens feel—with our overstocked medicine cabinets, burglar alarms, vast ghettos, and drug culture. Eighteen hundred New Yorkers are murdered every year by their fellow citizens in a city whose police department is larger than the standing army of many nations.[7]

When we try to bring freedom and liberty to other nations, we usually just trade one dictator and oppressive regime for another. We go to war in the name of liberating people from dictators, and frequently, the new leaders placed in power are just as corrupt and destructive as those who were removed. One group's quest for freedom often leads them to kill, enslave, and destroy countless others who are viewed as standing in the way of the first

---

[6] Most people prefer security over liberty and will sacrifice all sorts of liberties for the sake of peace, safety, and comfort. Liberty is the luxury of the secure. See Jacques Ellul, *The Subversion of Christianity* (Grand Rapids: Eerdmans, 1986), 168. This is one reason why security is a prominent topic in Scripture. Without security, there is no Christian liberty. Only with divine security are we truly free.

[7] Stanley Hauerwas and William H. Willimon, *Resident Aliens* (Nashville: Abingdon, 1989), 50.

group's liberty and freedom. Yet as soon as this new group of freedom fighters comes into power, they almost immediately begin to enslave and subjugate those who stand against them or oppose their rule.

Take any war, any struggle, or any fight by any nation or any group of people in the history of the world, in which their goal was liberty and freedom, and you will find countless atrocities, murders, and crimes, all committed in the name of liberty.

It is ironic that the Statue of Liberty, as the primary symbol of liberty in the United States, is a pagan goddess.[8] I fear that in our American quest for liberty, we have far too often followed a false goddess, rather than the true source of our freedom and liberty, Jesus Christ. When liberty is sought outside of the bounds of obedience to Jesus Christ, liberty becomes the cruelest taskmaster of all.

One of the people put to death during the French Revolution was a woman by the name of Madame Roland. On the way to the guillotine, she passed a large statue of the goddess Liberty (the same goddess portrayed by the Statue of Liberty in New York Harbor), and spoke these famous words: "O Liberty! What crimes are committed in thy name!" What crimes indeed!

Aside from the wars, revolutions, and genocides committed in the name of national liberty, there have been innumerable crimes

---

[8] The same is true, by the way, with the Washington Monument, the American Eagle, and numerous other central symbols of American Freedom, Liberty, and Justice. Nearly all American symbols have their roots not in Scripture, but in Egyptian, Babylonian, Greek, and Roman idol worship. I sometimes think we may have more idols than Athens (cf. Acts 17:22-23).

committed by individuals in the name of personal liberty. More often than not, what is meant by "freedom" is "freedom from accountability" or "freedom from consequences." People do not want to answer to anybody for what they do, least of all to God. They want guidance from nothing but their own conscience and desires so they can be free to make their own decisions and do what they want, regardless of the consequences to other people. When things go wrong in their life, they want to blame everybody else but themselves.

People seek the "freedom" to leave their marriages, abandon their children, operate their business for profit and greed, eat as much as they want, spend their time how they want, and treat other people with disdain and neglect. The excuse of "personal freedom" often results in decadence, selfishness, greed, gluttony, self-centeredness, sexual-immorality, misuse of money, mistreatment of others, and a wide variety of other sins of the flesh.[9]

Worst of all, the one beacon of light in this world for true liberty and freedom has been dimmed and dulled by those entrusted to carry it. True liberty comes only through the gospel of Jesus Christ, but the church has far too often been an accomplice and supporter of crimes committed in the name of liberty. We have cheered our nation on in its struggle for national and personal freedom against true or imagined enemies at home and abroad. When it comes to the personal freedom of the people in our pews, we are eager to encourage selfish and greedy living if it increases the bodies in the pews, the bucks in the offering plate, and

---

[9] Boyd, *The Myth of a Christian Religion*, 85.

the bricks on our building expansion.[10]

Today's "liberty" is no longer liberty, but has become a license to barbaric living. In chasing after freedom, we have become slaves to a master that devours and demands. Such freedom forces others to comply with our desires against their will. In exerting our own freedom, we restrict and remove freedom from others.[11] Sometimes we go so far as to kill those whom we view as threats to our selfish freedom, even going so far as to make public calls from the pulpits in our country to call for the obliteration and destruction of whole groups of people in other parts of the world because we view them as a threat to our way of life.[12] As C. S. Lewis suggested in his book, *The Great Divorce,* in our utopian quest for individualistic freedom, we find ourselves in a hell of isolation.

Over the centuries, the striving for liberty and freedom has become a religion unto itself, surpassing and overcoming most of the values and principles of Jesus Christ and His Kingdom.

> Like all religions, this religion has its own distinctive, theologized, revisionist history (for instance, the "manifest destiny" doctrine whereby God destined Europeans to conquer the land). It has its own distinctive message of salvation (political freedom), its own "set apart" people group (America and its allies), its own creed ("we hold these truths to be self-evident"), its own distinctive enemies

---

[10] See Jeremy Myers, *Church is More than Bodies, Bucks, & Bricks* (Dallas, OR: Redeeming Press, 2014).

[11] Ellul, *The Subversion of Christianity,* 166.

[12] Jerry Falwell once said, "You've got to kill the terrorists before the killing stops. And I'm for the president to chase them all over the world. If it takes ten years, blow them all away in the name of the Lord."

(all who resist freedom and who are against America), its own distinctive symbol (the flag), its own distinctive god (the national deity we are "under," who favors our cause and helps us win our battles). This nationalistic religion co-opts Christian rhetoric, but it in fact has nothing to do with real Christianity, for it has nothing to do with the kingdom of God.[13]

Responding to the siren call of freedom with liberty and justice for all, much of the American church has abandoned our loyalty to the example and teachings of Jesus, and fell head-over-heels in love with the goddess Liberty. And despite her name, she has proven to be a cruel mistress, especially when her power is threatened.

The seduction of liberty and freedom is so compelling because there is so much truth to it. It is true that people long for freedom. It is true that people deserve to be free. It is true that God created us to be free. It is true that Jesus Christ came to bring liberty and freedom, and that where the gospel of Jesus Christ is taught and lived, freedom and liberty grow and expand. The freest countries in the world and in history are those that have been influenced by the gospel of Jesus Christ.

The deception comes in when we think we can experience true liberty and freedom apart from Jesus Christ and the values of His Kingdom. There is no freedom or liberty apart from Jesus Christ. One of the central truths of the gospel is that we are enslaved to sin (John 8:34-36; Luke 4:18-19; Romans 6–7). This

---

[13] Gregory A. Boyd, *The Myth of a Christian Nation* (Grand Rapids: Zondervan, 2005), 150.

bondage cannot be broken in any other way than through the power of Jesus' death and resurrection. It is death that destroys the power of sin, and it is resurrection that grants a new life for the future.

Yet the gospel of Jesus Christ does not lead to complete freedom *the way the world defines it*. While the world defines freedom as the right to do whatever you want, the gospel defines freedom as laying down our freedom to serve the needs of others. Furthermore, the gospel frees us from the necessity of serving sin so that we are free to serve others. This is the paradox of the gospel which is often ignored by modern churches. Jesus Christ does not set us free so we can live any way we want. Jesus sets us free so we can follow Him into the world to be His hands and feet in loving acts of service to others.

Through His words and example, Jesus taught us to give up our liberties so that we might serve others. If we love others, we will become like a servant to them, putting their needs before our own, seeking to love and honor them with our time and energy. On the night Jesus was betrayed, He showed His disciples the full extent of His love by taking the form of a servant and washing their feet (John 13:1-17). The Apostle Paul understood this as well, which is why he so often referred to Himself as a bondservant of Jesus Christ (Rom 1:1; Php 1:1; Titus 1:1).

The personal and moral freedom that is so often taught in our churches is not part of the gospel, was not taught by Jesus Christ, and is in direct contrast to much of what the Scriptures teach. To the contrary, "personal liberty is something Kingdom people are called to *revolt* against."[14] The gospel calls us to give up our liberty, and sacrifice our freedom for the sake of serving and loving others. We need to reject freedom as the ultimate social goal.[15] Jesus gave up His right to liberty so He could serve others, and He calls those who follow Him to do the same.

If we want to be truly free, we must die to our right to liberty and understand that just as God limited His own freedom in creating a universe so that He might love His creation by serving it, so also, freedom is only free when our personal freedom is sacrificed for the freedom of others. As Jesus showed us time and time again in His ministry, true freedom is a freedom that serves.

RIGHT TO THE PURSUIT OF HAPPINESS

When the founding fathers wrote about the pursuit of happiness, they had something else in mind than what is often thought of today. The central idea behind the Declaration of Independence is that governments should follow the example of God in respecting individuals to make their own decisions. As long as a citizen lived their life in such a manner, they could reasonably expect to receive no interference from the government and, if their plans were successful, would achieve the dreams and goals they had for their life. They believed that the government should treat every-

---

[14] Boyd, *The Myth of a Christian Religion*, 86. Cf. also, Boyd, *The Myth of a Christian Nation*, 149.

[15] Stanley Hauerwas, *After Christendom? How the Church is to Behave if Freedom, Justice, and a Christian Nation are Bad Ideas* (Nashville: Abingdon, 1991), 50ff.

one equally and fairly under the law, and not hinder anybody's ability to pursue that which would give their life meaning and significance. The right to pursue happiness was the right to be more than a serf, a slave, or a tax-paying citizen, if that is what you wanted. The American Dream is founded on the idea that with hard work, discipline, and good choices, you can become anything you want to be.

I am not certain that this idea is exactly found in Scripture, but regardless of what the original founders thought about the pursuit of happiness, and whether or not it is actually taught in Scripture, the pursuit of happiness is not what people pursue today. Instead, in the name of "happiness," they pursue pleasure and personal fulfillment, even when such things come at the expense of others. Today, the pursuit of happiness and personal pleasure is nothing more than hedonism.[16]

This is not just a societal trait either. Such hedonistic thinking has infiltrated the church as well. Many Christians today make decisions, not based on what Scripture teaches, on what is right or wrong, or on how their decision will affect other people, but based solely on whether or not it will make them personally "happy" (however they define it). One of the more frequent sentences heard in pastoral counseling situations is "God wants me to be happy, right?" Husbands give this as a reason for divorcing their wife for another woman, college kids use it as an explanation for taking drugs or sleeping around, and businessmen use it to defend greed, lavish vacations, and shady corporate ethics. The

---

[16] Boyd, *The Myth of a Christian Religion*, 87.

pursuit of happiness is used as a justification to live any way they want and make whatever decisions they want, even if these choices will hurt and harm other people.

As with life and liberty, the Scripture does talk about happiness. But biblical happiness is derived from obeying God and serving others, even when such things result in personal pain, suffering, and maybe even death. Godly happiness is not self-serving, but is self-sacrificial. When we strive to live in the freedom for which we have been set free, so that we can become whom God made us to be, we will not live selfishly, seeking our will above all others while asking them to pay for our needs, desires, and wants. Instead, we will live with self-discipline, self-control, and self-sacrifice, as we put aside our needs to serve the needs of others. We will not demand that people pay our way through life, but will rather look for opportunities to help pave the way for others. The Spirit-directed life is not an entitled life, but is a life of gratitude for what we've been given and generosity toward those who have less. It is here where satisfaction and happiness are found.

Jesus, as in all things, is the perfect example. We cannot say that Jesus was unhappy, as He was probably the most perfectly joyous and fulfilled person the world has ever seen. Yet by modern definitions, Jesus certainly was not too intent on pursuing pleasure or fulfilling His own needs at the expense of others. Quite to the contrary, the entirety of Jesus' birth, life, and death was full of humility, pain, suffering, tragedy, and self-sacrifice. Jesus lived His life, not for Himself, but completely for the sake of others.

The early church understood what Jesus taught, and followed it in their own practice as well. In the early chapters of Acts, we

CERTAIN UNALIENABLE RIGHTS 137

read that those who had more possessions and money shared with those who had less (cf. Acts 2:44; 4:34-37). Some people today like to point to these passages as evidence that the Bible supports Communism, but note that what the early church did is quite different than what Communism demands. Communism says, "What's yours is mine, so give it to the government and they will distribute it equally among others." Christianity, however, says, "What's mine is yours, so let me help you when you are in need so that you can then help others." The Bible does not instruct Christians to give their money to the government through taxation so that the government can redistribute the wealth. The example of Jesus and the early church calls Christians to be voluntarily generous with their *own money* by giving it to those who need it and are deserving of it.

That last point is important. The Bible does not encourage laziness. When the Bible encourages Christians to financially support individual people who need and deserve the help, this support is never thought to be an entitlement or life-long "free ride." It is to help others in their time of need so that they can then rise up to their potential and work to support others (2 Thess 3:10). Even widows, who were not allowed to work at that time, were expected to contribute in some tangible way to the needs and ministries of the church (1 Tim 5:3-16).

So according to Scripture, happiness is not found in forcing others to pay for our way of life, or even in making sure our own dreams and pursuits are fulfilled at the expense of others. Instead, we are to personally live and work toward what God has called us to do, while also voluntarily sacrificing of our own time and energy to help others within our sphere of relationships. If we are going to live out the gospel, we must give up our right to pursue our own personal definition of happiness, and instead put the needs and rights of others first, seeking to love and serve them for their happiness, instead of asking them to serve us for ours.

CONCLUSION

Some might object to the content of this chapter by saying that if we do what is suggested in the previous pages, we will be defeated by our enemies, conquered by our foes, and taken advantage of by those who wish us harm. These are valid concerns. What good is it to give up our rights for the sake of the gospel if this allows others to prohibit our freedom to practice Christianity, share the gospel with others, meet in churches, and defend ourselves against violence?

It is these questions that we will seek to answer in the next chapter, as we look at how Christians should view the Bill of Rights, and specifically, the Freedom of Religion, the Right to Free Speech, the Right to Assemble, and the Right to Bear Arms.

DISCUSSION QUESTIONS

1. No government should try to take the "Unalienable Rights" which have been bestowed upon us by God. Yet we can voluntarily give up these rights. What would be the purpose for doing so?

2. What is the "deeper magic" that God built into creation? Do you know where the author heard this concept? (Hint: It comes from *both* C. S. Lewis and J. K. Rowling)

3. What are some ways in which you may be sacrificing your children or loved ones for the sake of your own dreams and desires? Be honest, for this is where the healing begins.

4. Who are people that you are most likely to shun and condemn? How do you think God views them?

5. Our Right to Life is really only ours to claim when we _____ for others.

6. Define what this chapter said about our Right to Liberty.

7. Whenever we cherish or desire a certain "Right" above God, what does that Right become?

8. When people speak of their Right to Freedom or Liberty, what are they usually speaking about?

9. What does Christ set us free to do?

10. Are pleasure and happiness synonymous? Why or why not?

CHAPTER 4

BILL OF RIGHTS

The Bill of Rights consists of the first ten amendments to the Constitution of the United States of America. These ten amendments, however, are not unique to the United States. Many of them were based on similar rights established in the constitutions and governing documents of other countries around the world, such as the British Bill of Rights of 1689.

The Bill of Rights of the United States was critically important for its founding as a free nation. The Constitution of the United States, while an impressive document, failed to put any meaningful limits on the control or power of the government. While the Constitution set up a system of checks and balances for the government and stated what the government should be doing, it did not adequately put limits upon the government or state what the government could not do. Several of the founding fathers of the United States sought to correct this weakness by proposing ten amendments to the Constitution called "The Bill of Rights." These were adopted by a majority of states in 1791 and became the law of the land.

Yet despite the critical importance of the Bill of Rights, an alarming number of citizens in the United States today have very little knowledge about what the Bill of Rights contains, or what it guarantees them under the law. A recent study on the Bill of Rights was conducted by the Bill of Rights Institute, and they learned that less than one-third of United States adult citizens knew what the Bill of Rights was, and fewer still knew what sort of protections were found within the Bill of Rights.

Most alarming of all, when asked to select some of what the Bill of Rights guarantees from a list of statements, 42 percent of American adults chose "from each according to his ability, to each according to his needs," which comes not from the United States Bill of Rights, but from Karl Marx's explanation of communism (See his "Critique of the Gotha Program").

Nevertheless, there are some statements in the Bill of Rights which almost everybody knows, and which many Christians often rely upon to defend themselves and the practice of Christianity. These rights which almost everybody knows about are found in the first two amendments of the Bill of Rights, and include the Freedom of Religion, the Freedom of Speech, the Freedom to Assemble, and the Freedom or Right to bear arms.

These "rights" or "freedoms" are often used as trump cards by some Christians as justification for saying and doing the meanest and most un-Christians things imaginable. We sometimes use the freedom of religion or the freedom of speech to say disparaging and rude things about other people. We defend our right to assemble whenever and wherever we want, even if it severely inconveniences others. And we sometimes use the right to bear arms to instill fear upon others or even to commit violence in the name of God.

I am so thankful to live in a country that has the sort of freedoms listed in the Bill of Rights. The freedoms and rights we enjoy are almost unparalleled in world history. Nevertheless, it sometimes seems that when Christians stand up for our rights, we do so in ways that do not look much like Jesus. Even though we may win legal battles in the defense of our rights, we sometimes lose the battle for the gospel of Jesus Christ. Our legal rights, as important as they are, sometimes get in the way of loving others like Jesus. When this happens, followers of Jesus need to have the courage to die to our rights rather than defend them. Sometimes, as followers of Jesus, living for others means dying to our rights.

> There is, in a very real sense, a way in which the idea of individual freedom and personal liberties is a myth. This type of freedom is ultimately false and deceptive, and points us not to God, who demands our lives, but to Satan, who tells us that our lives are ours to do with what we please.[1]

The following pages will look at four statements from the Bill of Rights that Christians often stand upon as justification for how we practice Christianity, and will invite us to consider how we might lay down these rights for the sake of others and the cause of the gospel. Let us begin with the Freedom of Religion, or the right to practice our religion any way we want.

RIGHT TO PRACTICE RELIGION

I am glad that I live in a country that offers the freedom of reli-

---

[1] Tripp York and Justin Barringer, eds., *A Faith Not Worth Fighting For* (Eugene, OR: Wipf & Stock, 2012), 92.

gion. It would not be pleasant to live where I would be fearful for my life and liberty simply for owning a Bible or gathering with other believers to pray and worship God. Living in a country where we have the freedom to believe what we want about God and worship God as we see fit is a great privilege and blessing.

I also love it that we do not have a government-endorsed religion. That is, I am glad that we do not live in a country where those who have political power tell us what religion we must belong to. There are countries today, as there have been throughout time, which outlaw the practice of all religion except the one that is sanctioned and approved by the government. In such situations, the government-approved religion is usually little more than the mouthpiece and enforcer of government policies and regulations.

So the freedom of religion that we enjoy in the United States today is a freedom I cherish and value. But does this mean that the freedom of religion is a guaranteed right? We often talk about the freedom of religion, but is this the same thing as the right to practice our religion?

The first amendment to the Constitution contains these words: "Congress shall make no law respecting an establishment of religion, or prohibiting the free exercise thereof." Since this amendment is part of what is known as "The Bill of Rights" many people believe that the freedom of religion is a "right." We demand this right, fight for this right, and sue other people and organizations whom we feel infringe upon this right.

I am not a Constitutional scholar, but let us consider the idea of the "freedom of religion" from several angles. Let us look at it from the historical-political, theological, and practical perspectives.

First, let us look at the freedom of religion from a historical and political perspective. The section of the First Amendment to the Constitution which deals with religion is known as "The Establishment Clause." It says that congress will make no law respecting an *establishment* of religion. Politicians, theologians, judges, and Constitutional lawyers have debated for centuries what exactly this means, for it is from this statement that people get the idea about "the separation of church and state."[2]

Most people today believe that the separation of church and state is a good idea. I suppose it is, because we are fallen human beings, and whenever a group of people get too much power, especially the combined powers of government and religion, such a combination of powers is usually accompanied by the terrible abuse of that power. We see this in countries today where there is no separation of church and state. Where the government controls the religion (such as in China and most of the Middle East), there is great abuse by the government upon people who want to practice a religion different than those allowed by the state. So separating the two powers of government and religion creates checks and balances for each, and allows greater freedom for the people who wish to follow the spiritual dictates of their heart.

However, from a theological perspective, the idea of the sepa-

---

[2] Strictly speaking, the idea of "the separation of church and state" is not in the constitution. Most people think it is, but the constitution says nothing of the sort. It simply has the Establishment Clause, which is *interpreted* in various ways, one of them being "the separation of church and state." Even this, however, is sufficiently ambiguous to be applied in various ways.

ration of church and state is not biblical. In biblical times, government and religion were always interwoven, and even the eventual government of Jesus will be a Theocracy, a complete and perfect intertwining of government and religion. The idea of the separation of church and state resulted from Enlightenment ideals in response to how religion is often used by government to dominate and control its citizens and make war on other nations.

Even from a practical standpoint, a case can be made against the freedom of religion and the separation of church and state. If one looks throughout the world and throughout history, the places and eras where Christianity is the most vibrant, faithful, effective, and Spirit-led, are the places where Christianity is illegal. It seems that when governments put their stamp of approval on Christianity as a religion, or when governments step back and allow people to worship as they see fit, it is then that Christian vibrancy and faithfulness suffers.

In light of all this, we should become quite troubled whenever Christian pastors and leaders call upon Christians to "take over" the government. If history is any guide, whenever Christianity becomes the state religion, violence, war, bloodshed, and injustice is sure to follow. Some of the bloodiest and cruelest eras in world history have occurred when Christianity gained the power of the state and became the official religion of the government. The crimes that are committed in the name of Christ by "Christian governments" are some of the worst the world has ever seen.

This is because—as Greg Boyd points out in his book, *The Myth of a Christian Nation*—Christianity was never intended to have "power over" others, but is based upon "power under" others.[3] Christianity is based on service, humility, self-sacrifice, and love. It is not based upon controlling, dominating, and ruling others. When Christianity gains power over others, it gains the very things which Satan offered to Jesus, and which Jesus rejected (Luke 4:1-13). When the church falls to these temptations, the church becomes more a tool of Satan than of the Savior.

The most ironic element in all of this, however, is that when the church demands and fights for its right to practice Christianity as we think we should, where do we go to protect and defend this right? We go to the government! In asking the government to affirm our right to practice religion by rulings from the courts and laws of this land, we have placed ourselves in bondage to the government. If separation of church and state is true, then the church does not need the state for approval. By going to the state through the courts and the legal law-system, we undermine the very thing we are trying to protect, namely, our desire to worship God apart from the interference of the state!

It could be argued, of course, that we are only trying to use "the laws of the land" to protect ourselves from the "laws of the land." Government, in its never-ending quest for more power and control, often tries to seize this power and control away from religion. Religion, it is argued, must defend itself from this encroachment by using the laws which the government respects and follows. But again, by using these laws, we often undermine the

---

[3] See Gregory A. Boyd, *The Myth of a Christian Nation* (Grand Rapids: Zondervan, 2005), 57f.

very independence and separation from government we seek to uphold.

But it gets worse. The way Christianity is most often practiced in the United States today (and other Western countries), we need the permission of the governments to continue practicing as we do. We depend on zoning laws for our buildings and parking lots. We depend on tax-exemptions to make our mortgage payments. We depend on 501(c)3 non-profit status to receive charitable donations and income. If the government stepped in and did away with just these three things, but did not make Christianity "illegal," I fear that most Christian churches would fold. Despite our claims to the contrary, Western Christianity often depends upon zoning laws, tax-exemptions, and 501(c)3 status for survival. In other words, we depend upon the government for our livelihood.

Think about it. How long would the average church survive if the government revoked the zoning ordinances and tax-exempt status for our buildings and property, and the 501(c)3 status for our donations? Most churches could not survive without them.

The situation would become more dire still if the government actually made Christianity illegal. If the government put out a law next week saying that Christianity was illegal, and Christians could no longer meet in church buildings on Sunday morning, could not sing songs, pray, or listen to sermons without fear of imprisonment, what would most Christians do? There would be three responses.

First, I fear that a significant number of Christians would simply stop practicing Christianity. The threat of being arrested for owning a Bible, meeting with other Christians for worship, or telling other people about Jesus would cause large numbers of Christians to simply walk away from the faith. "The law is the law," they would say. Besides, for most nominal Christians, going to church or practicing their religion didn't make that much of a difference in their life anyway, so why risk imprisonment for something that can just as easily be had through the Kiwanis Club or a Bowling League?

A second segment of Christianity—probably the vast majority of Christians—would fight. It probably wouldn't come to violence, but many thousands of churches, denominations, and leaders would lawyer up. We would probably see various denominations and church groups unite on this issue even though they have never before worked together on anything. Why? Because Christianity (as it is commonly practiced today) requires Sunday morning church services in church buildings, complete with public prayer, congregational singing, and pastoral preaching. In the minds of most, if you do not have these things going on, you do not have church. So many would fight.

Then there is the third segment of Christianity. These people would read the new law from the government, shrug their shoulders, and keep doing what they have been doing all along. This group knows that large public gatherings in buildings on Sunday mornings for preaching and singing are not essential to following Jesus. This group recognizes that we do not need nor require the permission of governments to live like Jesus in the world. This group of Christians knows that no law has ever been written, nor ever will be written, against what it looks like when people follow Jesus in their day-to-day lives. Those who simply follow Jesus live lives of love, joy, peace, patience, kindness, goodness, faithfulness, gentleness, and self-control. Against such things there is no law (Gal 5:23).

Since these are the three main ways Christians would respond to governmental infringement upon the freedom of religion, and among these three, only the third group is likely to survive unchanged, this raises the question if it might not be best to practice Christianity in the pattern of that third group regardless of whether or not there is freedom of religion. Maybe it is best to die to our right to practice religion according to the government's rules, and instead, follow Jesus in ways that do not need political permission or the decisions of the courts, and in ways against which no human government will ever raise a law.

When it comes to the freedom of religion, we can thank God that we live in a country where we have this freedom, but we must be careful how we go about trying to maintain it. Trying to maintain our religion of freedom may be counterproductive, for doing so requires us to petition the government for it, which leads people to believe that freedom of religion is subject to the will of those who govern. Furthermore, when we look to the government for the other religious freedoms which the government grants— such as the freedom to collect tax-free tithes, the freedom to assemble, and the freedom to say whatever we want—we become dependent upon the government for how we practice our religion, which then threatens our beliefs and practices if the government ever revokes such freedoms.

Thankfully, there is a way of following Jesus which does not depend upon the permission of the political class. We do not need laws about tax-exemption or freedom of speech in order to follow Jesus. In fact, depending on such things may actually lead us *away* from the values of Jesus and the Kingdom of God. Stanley Hauerwas put it this way:

> Freedom of religion is a temptation, albeit a subtle one. It tempts us as Christians to believe that we have been rendered safe by legal mechanisms. It is subtle because we believe our task as Christians is to support the ethos necessary to maintaining the mechanism. As a result, we lose the critical skills formed by the gospel to know when we have voluntarily qualified our loyalty to God in the name of the state.
>
> ... The question is not whether the church has the freedom to preach the gospel in America, but whether the church in America preaches the gospel as truth. The question is not whether we have freedom of religion and a corresponding limited state in America, but whether we have a church that has a people capable of saying no to the state. No state, particularly a democratic state, is kept limited by constitutions, but rather states are limited by people with the imagination and courage to challenge the inveterate temptation of the state to ask us to compromise our loyalty to God.[4]

In other words, by looking to the state to affirm our right to practice religion, we have sacrificed our ability to be the voice of conscience to the state. When we depend on the government for our freedom of religion, we effectively become a government chaplain in the pay of the state, and therefore, afraid of losing our jobs if we offend our employer by what we say or what we do.

---

[4] Stanley Hauerwas, *After Christendom? How the Church is to Behave if Freedom, Justice, and a Christian Nation are Bad Ideas* (Nashville: Abingdon, 1991), 71.

By seeking the endorsement of the state, we cannot adequately preach and teach the truth of the gospel because this truth will offend the state. Since the state provides us with our moral and legal right to exist, we limit the truth of the gospel to spiritual platitudes about what happens to people after they die, or how to be good tax-paying citizens with happy marriages and productive lives. Meanwhile, we must ignore the vast majority of the gospel message which criticizes the powers that be and calls them back to obedience to the will of God.

When we exist by the permission of the state, we must turn a blind eye to the many abuses of that state, and how it robs the poor, silences the minority, and marginalizes the victim. When the government grants us the power of existence, we must allow injustice to go unchallenged so that we may continue to exist. Seeking to live in the government's good graces almost guarantees that we will ignore the gospel message of God's grace, which issues a direct challenge to all dominions, powers, and authorities.

We have sacrificed the truth of the gospel on the altar of political influence, and have traded the power of sacrificial service in the name of Jesus Christ for the power of being the moral majority and voting in the candidates whom we think will champion our political cause. When we ask the government to defend our freedom of religion, we have almost no choice but to defend the government in return when they call upon us to endorse and defend their actions against others.

The church must choose between political persuasion and the gospel truth. We must choose between power politics and the Kingdom of God. Jesus calls us to take up our cross and follow Him in sacrifice and service, not because this is the most effective and influential way to change the world for the better, but simply because this is the way of the gospel. It is the way of God. It is the way of Jesus Christ. When we live this way, our lives and goals do not change when Kings die or new presidents are elected. Our lives and goals do not change if we live in an Atheistic, Communist country, a Muslim country, or a "Christian" country. Our ability to follow Jesus is not determined by the laws of religion within our country, but by the example of Jesus and the values of the Kingdom of God.

Do you want to follow Jesus? Don't look to the government for permission. You do not need the politically-granted right to the freedom of religion in order to love and serve others in Jesus' name. So don't run after freedom of religion. While we have it, accept it and thank God for it. But if the freedom of religion is taken away, don't fight for it. Instead, die to your right, and continue to live for Jesus.

RIGHT TO FREE SPEECH

In many places of the world, people have to be careful about what they say, and to whom they say it, especially when talking about their government. People who live in most Western nations generally do not have this fear. We have the right to publically state our opinion about what our leaders are doing, and may even disagree with or mock decisions our government officials make. This is a wonderful and amazing freedom which has rarely existed in history. Those in power usually do not like to hear dissent from those who have less power, and often take steps to silence those who disagree.

Certainly, there are some areas where the freedom of speech is restricted, such as shouting "fire" in a movie theater, talking about bombs on an airplane, and all forms of hate speech against people of other races or religions. But beyond this, the freedom of speech is a valuable right that we enjoy, and which, at least in the United States, is guaranteed by the First Amendment to the Constitution.

But just as with all the other rights in the Constitution, our right to the freedom of speech can be abused, especially when divorced from godly values and perspectives. When people lose their respect for others, and stop believing that all people have basic human dignity and value, the freedom of speech can become a curse. When the freedom of speech is divorced from God, people feel they have the right to say any mean and nasty thing they want about other people, simply because they have the freedom of speech. Apart from the values of God, free speech often degenerates into hate speech, and the right to free speech is used as an excuse to slander, gossip, ridicule, and condemn others.

Most tragically of all, the church is not immune to such abuses of the right to free speech. Some of the most hateful and hurtful things that can be said about other people and other religions are heard from our pulpits and in our books. There are numerous justifications we give for using such wounding words. Along with the freedom of speech, we feel that our position of being "right" allows us to publicly rebuke others, and say whatever we want about them, even if what we say is hurtful, slanderous, and mean-spirited.

But this is not the way of the gospel. This is not the way of Jesus. When zeal for the truth causes Christians to speak in mean and hurtful ways, we are justified in questioning whether such Christians really have the truth at all. The truth, when it is properly known, understood, and taught, will always be spoken with love toward other people. In speaking the truth in love, what matters is not how *you* think you are speaking, but how *others* think you are speaking. If they feel that what you said was not loving, then it probably wasn't. If truth cannot be spoken in love, then it is not truth. Love is never rude (1 Cor 13:5).

When it comes to speaking the truth in love, what matters is not how you think you are speaking; what matters is how others perceive it. I sometimes hear Christians say the meanest things to other people, and when confronted about it, they say "I am just saying what needs to be said to rescue their soul from hell. If you saw someone walking toward a cliff, wouldn't you shout and yell at them if it would keep them from walking off the cliff?"

I understand the analogy, but people walking off a cliff and people headed toward eternal separation with God are two very different things, and when God sought to rescue humanity from eternal separation, He did not yell at us, but instead sent Jesus, who loved and served others—including His enemies.

A quote from *The Myth of a Christian Nation* by Greg Boyd is particularly appropriate here:

> For the church to lack love is for the church to lack *everything.* No heresy could conceivably be worse!
>
> … We evangelical Christians often insist that we *are* loving; it's just that the world is so sinful they can't see it—or so we tell ourselves. *They* don't understand what "true love" is. That attitude is frankly as arrogant as it is tragic. … If contemporary people don't see in us

what ancient people saw in Christ, it can only be because the love that was present in Christ *isn't* present in us. And if they see in us what they saw in ancient Pharisees, it can only be because the self-righteousness found in the Pharisees *is* found in us.

Our comical insistence that we *are* loving, despite our reputation, is a bit like a man insisting he's a perfectly loving husband when his wife, kids, and all who know him insist he's an unloving, self-righteous jerk. If he persists in his self-serving opinion of himself, insisting that his wife, kids, and all who know him don't understand what "true love" is, it simply confirms the perspective these others have of him. This, I submit, is precisely the position much of the evangelical church of America is in. Until the culture at large instinctively identifies us as loving, humble servants, and until the tax collectors and prostitutes of our day are beating down our doors to hang out with us as they did with Jesus, we have every reason to accept our culture's judgment of us as correct. We are indeed more pharisaic than we are Christlike.[5]

People sometimes point to passages like Matthew 23 as justification for saying mean things to others. In this chapter, Jesus pronounces several "woes" upon the scribes and Pharisees, and also accuses them of many grave sins. In the process, He calls these Jewish teachers many names that sound mean and nasty. On one of my blog posts, I once had a person who disagreed with me lash out against me in a tirade of condemnatory name-calling. When I challenged Him on his lack of love, his only response was, "Jesus called people names; so can I."

---

[5] Boyd, *The Myth of a Christian Nation*, 134-135.

I will admit, it is hard to read love and kindness into Jesus' repeated accusation of these Jewish teachers being "hypocrites" (23:13, 14, 15, 23, 25, 27, 29), and also when He calls them "fools" (23:7) and a "brood of vipers" (23:33). None of this seems very loving, and in fact, some of it seems to flatly contradict Jesus' earlier instruction to not call anyone a fool (cf. Matt 5:22). So how can we understand this emotional outburst of Jesus in Matthew 23, and the exasperated name-calling He engages in throughout this impassioned speech?

Several things can help us understand Jesus' words. First, and most importantly, it is critical to remember that these words of Jesus in Matthew 23 were spoken against people of His own religious group. That is, Jesus was a Jewish teacher, and He was speaking against other Jewish teachers about areas of theological and behavioral disagreements. Jesus was not saying these things against other groups such as the Romans, the Samaritans, or some other group. This is an "in-house" debate.

Second, the impassioned statements of Jesus in Matthew 23 against the scribes and Pharisees only come after several years of receiving constant criticisms, condemnation, and judgment from the scribes and Pharisees. Jesus was not the instigator here. He is not seeking out people with whom He disagrees so that He can call them names and hurl insults in their general direction. No, Matthew 23 is one more part of an ongoing debate between Jesus and the religious leaders about who is properly understanding and applying the law of God.

Third, there are some cultural customs for Jesus' speech which we miss by being so far removed from the events of Matthew 23 by culture, language, geography, and time. For example, the term "hypocrite" is full of harsh and negative connotations today, but in the days of Jesus, it was a term used to refer to a stage actor who used a mask to hide his true face. If we were really going to use a cultural equivalent today, we might actually translate Jesus' use of the word "hypocrite" as "actor." Of course, this doesn't mean the word was positive. Though actors are often highly regarded in many modern Western cultures, Roman citizens usually viewed actors with disdain, especially when those in authority were thought to be "acting" in their public positions. Political and religious leaders were expected to speak honestly and do what they promised. Those who said one thing but did another were viewed only as "acting" out their public role, and therefore could not be trusted. This is how Jesus is using the term in Matthew 23. The scribes and Pharisees say one thing and do another, and so Jesus is calling them out as "religious actors."

The same sort of cultural background information helps us understand why He calls them serpents and a brood of vipers in Matthew 23:33. One of the Jewish High Priests in those days was Annas, and he was sometimes referred to as a "viper" for how he whispered and hissed into the ears of political rulers to influence and sway their decisions. When Jesus speaks of the "brood of vipers," this phrase could also be translated as "children of vipers," which may be a reference to Annas. In other words, Jesus is saying that these scribes and Pharisees were listening to and doing the bidding of Annas, the corrupt religious High Priest. So in calling them serpents and children of vipers, Jesus isn't just calling them names, He is informing them that He knows where their true loyalties lie. They are pawns of Annas, doing his bidding and listening to his lies.

Fourth, and maybe most important for our discussion here, I think the way we read texts like this is often more of a reflection of what is in our own heart than anything else. As an example, you can often determine a person's view of God by asking them to read 2 Samuel 12:1-7 out loud, with as much emotion as possible. When the person gets to 12:7, if they read Nathan's statement "You are the man!" with anger and hostility, then they very likely view God as angry and hostile toward sin. If, however, they read 12:7 with tears, sorrow, and pain in their voice, then they might understand that God is hurt by sin because He knows it hurts us.

I think that Matthew 23 is another sort of theological litmus test for how people view God. Despite how it is often read and taught in our churches, Matthew 23 can be read as an impassioned and sorrow-filled plea to the scribes and Pharisees to turn from their destructive theology and hypocritical behavior before it is too late. It is possible to read Matthew 23 with tears in your eyes instead of anger in your voice. And in fact, I think that Jesus' statement in Matthew 23:37 about how He has longed to gather the people of Israel under His wings like a mother hen protecting her chicks reveals the emotions that Jesus is feeling in the rest of the chapter. He is not angry. He is not being mean and rude. He is pleading, calling, and urging the religious leaders of Jerusalem to practice what they preach and to turn to God in true righteousness, justice, and mercy. Some Bible translations bring this out better than others. The New Living Translation, for example, does use the word "Woe" throughout Matthew 23, but instead translates it as "What sorrow awaits you."

Ultimately, Matthew 23 (and other texts like it) is not an example of where Jesus speaks meanly and rudely to other people or calls them names. Matthew 23 cannot be used by modern Christians as justification to say whatever we want to other people. It definitely cannot be used to defend the practice of condemning people outside the church who we think are "sinners." Jesus never had a negative thing to say about anyone who was outside of His own religious "house." He never condemned any other religion. He never condemned tax-collectors, prostitutes, or other sinners. He never said a word against homosexuality, even though it was rampant in Greco-Roman culture. If Christians are truly going to follow the example of Jesus, the only people we can justifiably criticize are other Christians, and even then, only those who are using "religion" to condemn others while making themselves look holy and righteous. It seems that the only sin Jesus was really upset about was the sin of religious pride. Everybody else of every other group which committed every other sin received nothing but love, grace, mercy, and forgiveness. Yes, Jesus called tax-collectors and prostitutes to stop sinning, but this was always and only after He had made it clear to them through His words and actions that He loved them, forgave them, and accepted them completely.

This is how Christians can practice our "freedom of speech." While our government may give us the freedom of speech and the right to say just about anything we want to anyone we want, the gospel of Jesus Christ gives us no such freedom. Our speech must always be with grace, as we speak the truth in love, making sure that in everything we say, no unwholesome word proceeds out of our mouth, but only what is beneficial, edifying, encouraging, uplifting, and helpful (Col 4:6; Eph 4:15, 29). Under the gospel, we do not have the right to say what we want, when we want, and where we want, but are called to speak in such a way that all people will be drawn to Jesus because of His great love for them as revealed in our words and actions. Until we are able to speak this way, we do not have the right to free speech, but only the right to remain silent.

And when we speak, we do so with truth and in love, knowing that there may be consequences for what we say, because the light of truth is rarely welcome in this world of darkness.

> True freedom is not having the right to say whatever you want without consequences; it is being able to say what is right regardless of the consequences.[6]

True freedom of speech is not about whether or not we have the right to say something, but rather about whether or not we are right in what we say, and if we fully accept and embrace the consequences of saying it. If we are truly going to practice our freedom of speech in Christ, we must be willing to speak the truth in love, fully knowing that doing so may lead to our death.

RIGHT TO ASSEMBLE

The freedom of assembly is another right guaranteed in the Constitution of the United States. Christians have sometimes used the freedom of assembly to defend their right to gather in church buildings and other public areas for the purpose of worship and

---

[6] York and Barringer, eds., *A Faith Not Worth Fighting For*, 98.

fellowship. It is unlikely that the founding fathers had religious assemblies in mind when they wrote about the right to peaceably assemble, for religious assemblies would more properly fall under the right to practice religion. The freedom of assembly more likely had in view the right of people to assemble for political reasons, such as for peaceable protests and demonstrations.

Nevertheless, the church has sometimes claimed the right to assemble for purposes that are contrary to the example of Jesus and the values of the gospel. Churches have sometimes used the freedom of assembly to obstruct the rights of other people. Some churches picket businesses which engage in practices the church condemns. Some churches try to hinder other groups of people from gathering to celebrate their lifestyle or religion. A few churches have even used the freedom of assembly for the purpose of interrupting funerals and blocking parades.

There are also churches that want to build a giant building right in the middle of a quiet residential area, and even though the entire community is upset about the traffic this mega church will cause during the nights and weekends, the church uses their freedom of assembly to defend their right to construct their building anywhere they please.

Christians would be wise to remember that one of the primary purposes for the existence of the church is so that we can be a blessing to the world. Yet when we assemble in some of the ways described above, we are more likely to be viewed as a curse than a blessing. People are more likely to associate us with screaming, yelling, fanatical sign-wavers, than with loving, serving, humble ministers of grace.

Though we do have a right to assemble in this country, but as followers of Jesus, we must be ready and willing to sacrifice that right for the sake of others. Our true assembly as the Body of Christ is primarily a spiritual gathering in Christ. One truth of the gospel is that we are already assembled in Jesus Christ. So whether we gather in large groups or small, we can still know that we are assembled with all other saints around the world and throughout time.[7] And for this assembly, we need no permission from the government, nor do we need to fight for such a right. When we fight for our right to assemble, we turn the blessings of the gospel into a curse. To truly be a blessing to others, it may be best to die to our legal right to assemble, and instead, assemble as the Body of Christ to love, serve, help, and bless others.

RIGHT TO BEAR ARMS

The Constitutional right to bear arms is technically about the right of an individual to defend and protect themselves and their family against intruders and those who wish to do them harm. In general, I fully support this right, and believe that the Constitutional right to bear arms is valuable, important, and necessary in a world such as ours.

I do wonder, however, what Jesus would have thought about the right to bear arms and the subject of self-defense. After all, He would not even allow Peter to raise a sword in His defense (Matt 26:52), nor did He utter a word in self-defense at His trial when

---

[7] See Jeremy Myers, *Skeleton Church: The Bare Bones Definition of Church* (Dallas, OR: Redeeming Press, 2012).

false accusations were leveled against Him (Matt 27:12-14). But self-defense is a complex issue, and it is not primarily this issue that concerns me here.

My main concern is with what seems to be the duty and obligation of our churches to provide moral support for the wars of our nation against other countries and against some within our own borders. I get quite concerned when churches and church leaders preach and teach about our responsibility to kill, bomb, and destroy other people in the name of freedom and justice—or worse yet, in the name of Jesus. We see the evil and terror that goes on in other countries, and think that as the moral guardians of the world, it is our responsibility to bring evildoers to justice, and to right what is wrong in this world.

This seems honorable. Is it not the responsibility of those with power to use that power to protect the weak, and advance the cause of freedom and justice? Yes, it is. The problem, however, is when people use violence as the means by which they attempt to protect the weak and advance freedom and justice. One of the greatest myths in all of history is the idea that violence against others is the only way to stop the spread of violence. Nearly every book and movie contains this great myth, and almost everyone believes it, despite the fact that history has proven time and time again that violence will never put an end to violence. Yet nevertheless, we train our children in this myth from the moment they are born. Even most cartoons and children's books are based on the myth that violence must be used to defeat violence.[8]

Christians even developed the theory of "Just War" in which certain types of wars against our enemies were considered righteous, and as such, sanctioned by God. The "Just War" theory was originally developed by Augustine to defend the Empire's actions of arresting and killing the Donatists, with whom Augustine was having a theological disagreement. He argued that in certain situations, a war is not wrong if it furthers the cause of Christ and advances the Kingdom of God on earth. He taught that inflicting temporal pain on someone to help them avoid eternal pain was justified. Also, Augustine believed that since God sometimes uses terror for the good of humans (a questionable premise), the church may also use terror for the sake of the gospel.[9]

Thanks to Augustine, Christians have been endorsing wars against "Christian enemies" ever since. But does not the life of Jesus and the truth of the gospel cry out against this? "Declaring a war just is simply a ruse to rid ourselves of guilt."[10] Such attempts to absolve ourselves from guilt in the murder of others have been around since the very beginning.

The killing of others began in the very first family, when Cain killed Abel. And why did Cain commit the first murder? The Bible is rather vague about Cain's motives, but the root causes appear to be a mixture of jealousy, anger, and the desire for self-

[8] For the best discussion of the myth of redemptive violence, see Walter Wink, *Engaging the Powers: Discernment and Resistance in a World of Domination* (Minneapolis: Fortress, 1992).

[9] Boyd, *The Myth of a Christian Nation*, 78.

[10] Wink, *Engaging the Powers*, 225.

advancement. Cain was trying to give God's fruit back to Him so that God would let him and his family back into the Garden, but when God rejected Cain's offering in favor of Abel's, Cain murdered his brother.

We rightfully condemn Cain for his actions, but when we look at the situation from Cain's perspective, his murder of Abel was the very first "Just War" in history. Miroslav Volf points out that Cain's murder of Abel was governed by faultless logic, assuming his premises were true:

> Premise 1: "If Abel is who God declared him to be, then I am not who I understand myself to be."

> Premise 2: "I am who I understand myself to be."

> Premise 3: "I cannot change God's declaration about Abel."

> Conclusion: "Therefore, Abel cannot continue to be."[11]

From Cain's perspective, he had the duty and obligation to protect himself by murdering Abel. If he had admitted that God's preference for Abel's offering was correct, then Cain would have had to face his own faults. This he could not do, and so, in self-defense against the moral challenge from his brother, Cain engaged in "Just War" against Abel, and murdered him.

Nearly all "Just Wars" in history follow the same logic. We engage others in a righteous battle, defending our freedoms and

---

[11] Miroslav Volf, *Exclusion & Embrace: A Theological Exploration of Identity, Otherness, and Reconciliation* (Nashville: Abingdon, 1996), 95.

liberties, not because the others are necessarily evil and wrong (though we paint them in this light), but because the only alternative to "Just War" is to admit our own wrongdoing and faults. Since this is what we will not do, "the other" must die. It is either us or them. There has never been a war in history in which the warriors from both sides did not think their cause was just. In every battle, both sides cry out to their god for victory. Both sides defend their right to attack the other in self-defense.

Can we really believe as Christians that since we serve the one true God, our cause is more just than the causes of those we are trying to kill? Does it not rather seem that if we truly serve the one true God as revealed in Jesus Christ, that there would be no cause whatsoever for killing? When we seek the blood of our enemies, are we not abandoning and forsaking the truth of the shed blood of Jesus, who died *for* His enemies?

> Devotion to the way of Christ means that we do not take up worldly weapons of violence and power; we simply do as Christ did by laying down our lives rather than trusting in our own competency to "make things right."[12]

Many Christians, however, frequently call for the death of our enemies, pointing to various passages in Scripture for support. Among the more popular Scriptures are Genesis 6, the violence God commands in the books of Joshua and Judges, the pervasive bloodshed and violence in the Book of Revelation, and a text or two from the Gospels. A full-length book would be required to

---

[12] York and Barringer, eds., *A Faith Not Worth Fighting For*, 102.

explain the violence of these texts (which I am currently writing), but for now, since Jesus in the Gospels is the primary model for the church, and since our primary focus here is in relation to the Constitutional right to bear arms, let us look at one text from the Gospels which is often cited as justification for the Christian's right to bear arms.

Some point to Jesus' instructions to His disciples to sell their cloak and buy a sword (Luke 22:36) as evidence that Jesus defends the right to bear arms. I recently heard a conservative radio talk show host reference Luke 22:36 as evidence that Christians should do everything they possibly can to buy guns and ammunition. If Luke 22:36 is quoted out of context, this certainly seems to be what Jesus is endorsing. On closer inspection however, Jesus is teaching the exact opposite.

In Luke 22, the disciples do what Jesus instructs, and they come back with two swords. When Jesus sees them, He says, "It is enough" (Luke 22:38). But the question is "Enough for what?" Two swords among a ragtag band of fishermen and tax-collectors would accomplish nothing against the well-trained and highly-disciplined Roman army. Jesus wasn't saying, "Bring swords" so that He could defend "the right to bear arms." Nor did He say "It is enough" because He was going to miraculously multiply the two swords into thousands as He had done with the loaves and fishes. To the contrary, when Peter actually tries to use one of these swords a few verses later, Jesus scolds Him, tells Peter to put the sword away, and even heals the enemy that Peter had attacked (Luke 22:50-52). It is quite obvious from the events at this last night before His crucifixion that although Jesus told His disciples to bring swords, He had no intention of them using them against others. So why did He want them to bring the swords?

Luke explains why right in the context. In between the instruction of Jesus to go buy swords (Luke 22:36), and the statement of Jesus that two swords is enough (Luke 22:38), Jesus quotes from Isaiah 53:12 saying that He had to fulfill a prophecy which said He would be numbered among the transgressors (Luke 22:37). In other words, Jesus needed to appear as if He were a common criminal, a rebel, an insurrectionist. Jesus was not any of these things, but He had to appear as if He was to fulfill the prophecy of Isaiah 53:12, and for this, two swords was "enough." Since Jesus had no intention of using the swords to carry out violence upon others, we cannot use Luke 22 to defend our right to bear arms.[13]

Sadly, despite the clear teaching and example of Jesus, the Christian church seems far more eager to take up arms against our enemies than we are to take up our cross and follow Jesus in dying for our enemies.

> In the name of the one who taught us not to lord over others but rather to serve them (Matt 20:25-28), the church often lorded over others with a vengeance as ruthless as any version of the kingdom of the world ever has. In the name of the one who taught us to turn the other cheek, the church often cut off people's heads. In the name of the one who taught us to love our enemies, the church often burned its enemies alive. In the name of the one who taught us to bless those who persecute us, the church often became a ruthless

---

[13] After writing this section of this chapter, I found that Preston Sprinkle adopts a similar position in his book. See Preston Sprinkle, *Fight: A Christian Case for Non-Violence* (Colorado Springs: David C. Cook, 2013), 237.

persecutor. In the name of the one who taught us to take up the cross, the church often took up the sword and nailed others to the cross.[14]

Our world is soaked in blood as nation rises against nation. Far too often, the church has stood in support of their nation as it went off to war, defending the nation's righteous cause while calling for the blood of its enemies. How can this be when we have Jesus as our example? How can we possibly think that Jesus, who shed His blood for His enemies, would support our attempts to shed the blood of our enemies?

When President Truman dropped the first atomic bomb on Hiroshima in 1945, he turned to the group of sailors with him on the battle cruiser *Augusta*, and said, "This is the greatest thing in history."[15] Was the instant destruction of hundreds of thousands of lives more important than the redeeming self-sacrifice of Jesus Christ on the cross for the salvation of all mankind? Nevertheless, the vast majority of Christian churches in the United States supported and approved of President Truman's decision.

After the bomb, all sorts of moral compromises were easier—nearly two million abortions a year seemed a mere matter of freedom of choice, and the plight of the poor in the world's richest nation was a matter of economic necessity.

The project, begun at the time of Constantine, to enable Christians

---

[14] Boyd, *The Myth of a Christian Nation*, 81.

[15] Stanley Hauerwas and William H. Willimon, *Resident Aliens* (Nashville: Abingdon, 1989), 26.

to share power without being a problem for the powerful, had reached its most impressive fruition. If Caesar can get Christians [in Germany] to swallow the "Ultimate Solution," and Christians here to embrace the bomb, there is no limit to what we will not do for the modern world.[16]

The church must put up a limit. We must remind ourselves and the world that enough blood has been shed, that the last thing this world needs is more blood.

But instead, we go and kill our neighbors and our brothers, and we do it in the name of justice and freedom. We kill for the cause of Christ while the shed blood of Jesus cries out to us from the cross: *Enough!* For though we were His enemies, and He had the only "just cause" in history, He did not seek to defeat His enemy by putting us to death, but by facing death Himself. "When God flexes His omnipotent muscle, it doesn't look like Rambo or the Terminator—it looks like Calvary!"[17] The self-sacrificial love of Jesus on the cross was not only the way of redemption, reconciliation, and forgiveness for the whole world, but was also an example that we are called to follow in our own pursuit of peace and reconciliation with other people.

> The Kingdom of God has broken into human history, and while the nations still make war, the people of God embodies a new alternative. The mission of the church is to serve as an outpost of the coming peaceable Kingdom, putting away our former ways of war

---

[16] Ibid., 27.
[17] Boyd, *The Myth of a Christian Nation*, 32.

making.[18]

The never-ending cycle of violence will never stop through the use of more and greater violence, but through the self-sacrificial way modeled by Jesus.[19] It is as William Blake has said, "The glory of Christianity is to conquer by forgiveness." Yes. And I would add that we also conquer by prayer.

Though I write a lot of books and host an online discipleship group, my "day job" consists of working in a prison as a chaplain. On Friday afternoons, around 12:30, the Muslim community shows up in the chapel for their weekly Jumah prayer. On one particular Friday, 107 Muslim men had gathered for prayer, but as they were washing their feet and faces and laying out their prayer rugs, the prison authorities called me on the phone and told me to cancel the Jumah prayer service.

It is not wise to cancel Jumah prayer for any reason. But since there was a looming security concern in the prison, I had no choice, and went and informed the gathering Muslims.

The seething anger directed my way was palpable. All 107 Muslims stood up, glared at me, and started to gather around me

---

[18] York and Barringer, eds., *A Faith Not Worth Fighting For*, 142.

[19] The issue of justice, war, and following Jesus is a *huge* topic, and highly debated within Christian circles. I have no hope of even beginning to answer all the questions related to such a topic in a few short paragraphs. Instead, I direct you to a few books which have instructed and challenged my own thinking on this issue. Note that these books do not promote pacifism, which is not something I promote either. Instead, they define and defend a "Third Way" between violence and pacifism, a way that was taught by Jesus and modeled by such historical figures as Ghandi and Martin Luther King Jr. See Gregory A. Boyd, *The Myth of a Christian Religion* (Grand Rapids: Zondervan, 2009), chapter 8; Boyd, *The Myth of a Christian Nation*, chapters 4, 9; Wink, *Engaging the Powers*.

in a tight circle. I sensed that how I responded in the next few seconds would determine whether I lived or died that day.

"You can't cancel the Jumah prayer," said the Imam of the group. "It's mandatory. It's required."

"Yes, I know," I calmly responded. "But there is a security concern, and until it's resolved, everybody is required to return to their housing units." In a prison, security takes precedence over all things, even over religion. But even still, nobody likes to have their religious service cancelled.

"So what are we supposed to do, Chaplain?" asked the Imam. "Allah demands that we pray, but you are demanding we not pray. Who should we obey?"

The crowd of Muslims pressed in closer to hear how I would respond. My mind raced, and I knew that the security concern could quickly escalate into a security crisis (and possibly a riot) depending on the next words that came out of my mouth.

It is very difficult to practice nonviolence in a system that is inherently and purposefully built upon the principles of violence. The central principal of violence is that you get what you want by having a bigger stick. You might not always use the stick; most of the time, simply having the bigger stick is enough. This idea was immortalized in Teddy Roosevelt's famous explanation of his foreign policy: "Speak softly, and carry a big stick." As long as your stick is bigger than your enemy's, this should be enough to deter him from war.

The prison system is founded on this "big stick" principal. Prisons are places where people who have engaged in various forms of violence are forced to live in a place where they have very few sticks at their disposal, while all the guards and prison staff have much larger sticks. The big stick principal is what keeps the prison relatively safe and secure.

But the "big sticks" are not what you think. Despite the common perception, most prison staff in the west no longer carry weapons of any kind. Guards do not have guns or billy clubs. Prison staff are typically only "armed" with a radio. Outmanned and overpowered, modern prison guards are trained to use their minds and mouths to maintain peace inside a prison. But it doesn't always work. When it doesn't, riots break out, people are killed, and yes, sometimes the guns are brought in. Yet even then, only non-lethal munitions are used.

Working in the prison system as I do, I have found a "weapon" that is even more powerful than the radio. It is the constant "radio connection" I have with God. So as the Muslims angrily asked whether they should obey Allah or men, I quickly asked God for wisdom on what to say.

In that moment, Acts 5:29 flashed through my mind where Peter was faced with a similar dilemma, and stated, "We must obey God rather than men." This was my answer.

"You should pray," I said.

There was a collective gasp by the Muslims.

I could sense their thoughts. Was I mocking them? Or was I actually telling them to disobey an order?

But I continued. "Nobody is demanding that you not pray. I invite you to pray. I want you to pray. I ask you to pray. I hope that you will pray. But today, because of the security concern, you are going to have to pray down in your housing units. Allah is powerful, is he not? He will hear your prayers down in the unit just as well as he will hear them in this place. So pray to Allah that this security situation would be resolved quickly and peacefully. Then maybe we can get you back up here to the chapel a little later this afternoon for your communal Jumah prayer."

They started at me, still trying to decide how to respond.

I waited.

Finally, the Imam turned to the gathered Muslims and said, "The Chaplain is right. Allah can hear our prayers and work to resolve this situation quickly. We will return to our housing units."

Later that afternoon, I was indeed able to make arrangements for the Muslims to return to the Chapel for their afternoon Jumah prayer. It was late, but at least it was done. The Muslims praised Allah for hearing and answering their prayers, and I praised Jesus for answering mine. Prayer, and a commitment to maintain peace, helped resolve this potentially violent situation.

But do forgiveness, prayer, and non-violence actually work in the real world, to bring an end to real conflicts between countries? More specifically, can anyone believe that prayer, forgiveness, and a commitment to non-violence would have been effective in defeating the Nazis or defending ourselves against Al-Qaeda? Frankly, I myself don't believe it. Yes, prayer is powerful. But prayer is not a magic wand that ends wars.[20]

I'm not even sure that dialogue would have created peace in these situations. There are some well-meaning optimists in government and church leadership who seem to think that we can

---

[20] See my book, *What is Prayer?* (Dallas, OR: Redeeming Press, 2018) for some ideas on how prayer *could* work to end war.

create peace through dialogue and talk our enemies into not attacking us by apologizing for our own role in whatever disagreements we have. I have no such illusions. If the United States disbanded our military, decommissioned our nuclear weapons, and told the world we were sorry for all the hurt and pain we had caused through the centuries, this would not bring out world peace, but would simply mean that the United States would quickly fall to some dictatorial and militaristic regime, which would then turn around and use our people and our natural resources to turn their sights upon other nations and people.

But must we then constantly resort to the never ending expansion of the industrial military complex? Is it true, that despite what the Bible teaches and despite the example of Jesus, the only real way to peace in this world is to make sure you are stronger than the next guy (or government) so that they think twice before attacking? Was Teddy Roosevelt right when he said that the key to peace was to "Speak softly and carry a big stick"? If so, why did Jesus never carry a big stick?

It seems that maybe the problem lies in the fact that a false dichotomy has been presented to most people in most countries throughout time. People generally assume that in the face of violence, there are only two possible responses: fight or flight. Many assume that the only options are to either attack and kill or lie down and be killed; to either be a war hawk or a pacifist.

More confusing yet, both sides of the debate often enlist Jesus to defend their position. As proof for a stance on war, some point to Jesus' use of a whip to clear the temple, His instructions to His disciples to buy swords, and His future return on a war horse to exact vengeance on His enemies. The pacifist position, however, looks to Jesus' instructions to turn the other check, to love your enemies instead of hate them, and His refusal to defend Himself at His trial or on the cross.

The solution to the problem is to discover the middle way of non-violent resistance. Honestly, I do not know if it is possible for governments to operate with this approach, but it is a way for *individual* people and groups to live in a way that subverts the violent forces of a surrounding culture while refusing to resort to violence ourselves. Non-violent resistance is how Gandhi brought about change in India, and how Martin Luther King, Jr. changed the way America treated blacks. More importantly, non-violent resistance was modeled by Jesus Christ Himself.

Non-violent resistance allows a person to stand up for life, liberty, and the pursuit of happiness without denying these same rights to other people. In fact, non-violent resistance stands up for these rights for *both* the oppressor and the victims.

Though I do not have the time or space in this conclusion to fully explain non-violent resistance, let me present a few of the guiding principles of this practice, and also suggest a few books so you can do further reading and research on your own.[21]

During my years of working as a prison chaplain, I have found six principles that help me navigate the tricky and treacherous waters of practicing nonviolence in a system built on violence.

---

[21] The following six principles of non-violence are loosely based on what Dr. Martin Luther King, Jr. taught in his book, *Stride Toward Freedom: The Montgomery Story* (Boston: Beacon, 1958). See also my blog posts on Non-Violent Resistance: https://redeeminggod.com/non-violent-resistance/ and https://redeeminggod.com/nonviolent-resistance-and-pacifism/

The six principles form an acrostic for "CHRIST" because they are founded upon the teachings and example of Jesus Christ. Here are the six principles, with a brief explanation for each.

Creativity

The world trains people that when we are faced with violence, the best response is greater violence. In other words, we must fight fire with fire, or fight violence with greater violence. But the tragic reality is that violence always and only leads to more violence.

This means, therefore, that those who would practice non-violence must start to find creative, alternative solutions out of violent situations.

This is easier said than done, however, and so our attempts at creative responses must be bathed in prayer for God, the Creator, to guide us into creative non-violent responses as well. There is no "one size fits all" response to violence, for each situation is different and requires a different response. So creativity is required. But God can guide each of us into the creative responses that will bring peace to violent situations.

Honesty

It takes two to tango. It also takes two to fight. And have you ever noticed that in nearly every violent engagement, both sides think the other one "started it"? Even in the case of terrorists flying planes into skyscrapers, they thought that they were righteously responding to the unjust treatment of their people by the United States. Even Hitler believed he was responding to the unjust treatment of Germany after their losses in World War I.

So in any sort of violent engagement, we must be brutally honest with how we ourselves contributed to the problem. We must not and cannot place all the blame on the other person, for this will only cause greater problems.

Realism

Let's be realistic: non-violence doesn't always end violence. We live in an evil world, and sometimes, evil wins. So we must not think that non-violence always "works" and is the magic cure-all for everything that ails the world. It isn't. It doesn't always work. In fact, the opposite is often true. Those who practice non-violence often do get defeated, destroyed, or killed. Jesus is the prime example.

So why practice non-violence? Because even if non-violence rarely works, it is still better than violence, which never works. Violence always and only creates more violence. But sometimes, non-violence creates peace, and therefore, it has a better success rate. But we must be realistic and recognize that a non-violent response will not always bring an end to violence. It often won't.

Incarnation

If we want to practice non-violence, we must understand that we are incarnating Jesus to the world, just as He incarnated God to us. It is not we who are out there all on our own standing up for love, patience, forgiveness, and peace, but it is Jesus in us who is standing up for these things. Furthermore, the recognition that we are the incarnation of Jesus on earth encourages us to live as He lived and love as He loved.

With this realization that we are the incarnation of Jesus, this helps us choose love over hate. Since love is unmotivated, unselfish, creative, and always seeks the good of others, those who practice non-violence will return good for evil and forgiveness for hate.

Just like Jesus, non-violence seeks to win friendship and understanding from enemies. It does not seek to shame or humiliate enemies, but to redeem and reconcile them to us, and to each other. We will not seek to defeat people, but to defeat injustice. Non-violence recognizes that those who perpetrate violence are victims of violence as well, and need to be liberated from their bondage as well.

Strength

It is very easy to respond to violence with violence. People often talk about the courage and bravery of war, and indeed, it does take courage to charge onto the field of battle, not knowing if you will make it back off.

Similarly, while it does take great courage and bravery to pull a knife or a gun on an assailant, it takes even greater strength and courage to stand up to violence without engaging in violence.

It is much harder to take the blows that fall on your back without retaliating than to lash out and trade blow for blow. Non-violence is not weakness or cowardice, but takes the greatest strength and courage. It takes great spiritual, mental, and emotional strength to engage in non-violent resistance and must not be entered into lightly.

The way of non-violence is not for the weaklings; it can only be practiced and followed by the strongest and bravest among us.

Trust

If God is non-violent, and calls us to practice non-violence as well, then we must trust God to work in us and through us, even though our minds, wills, and bodies scream out in protest at the ways of non-violence.

It is only when we trust in God to bring a solution to a bad situation that God will step in to do exactly that. Despite the rhetoric of war, God is on the side of justice, not just for one party or another, but for all. Though it may take time, justice will always win.

And related to this, in light of the previous five principles, it important to know that even if we die while practicing non-violence, we can still trust God to use our death to create peace, just as He did in Jesus. A resolute trust in God reminds us that sometimes it is better to die than to kill.

Jesus modeled the way for us to live with non-violence toward others. Yes, we must resist evil wherever it is found, and we must stand up for righteousness and justice, but we must do so in the ways of Jesus, through non-violent resistance.

If you want to learn more about non-violent resistance, what it is, and how to practice it as a follower of Jesus, I recommend "The Powers Trilogy" by Walter Wink, *Fight* by Justin Sprinkle, and *A Faith Not Worth Fighting For,* edited by Tripp York and Justin Barringer.[22]

Let me close this chapter with a personal note. Although I accept that Jesus taught non-violent resistance and that this is the

---

[22] Preston Sprinkle, *Fight: A Christian Case for Non-Violence* (Colorado Springs: David C. Cook, 2013); Walter Wink, *Naming the Powers: The Language of Power in the New Testament* (Philadelphia: Fortress, 1984); Walter Wink, *Unmasking the Powers: The Invisible Forces that Determine Human Existence* (Philadelphia: Fortress, 1986); Walter Wink, *Engaging the Powers: Discernment and Resistance in a World of Domination* (Minneapolis: Fortress, 1992); York and Barringer, eds., *A Faith Not Worth Fighting For.*

only way to properly advance the rule and reign of God on earth, I know what lurks in my own heart, and I know that despite what I can write on a page or teach with my lips, if it comes to defending myself against violent men, or worse yet, defending my wife and children from attackers, I will most likely resort to violence. There is a vast difference between accepting the truth of an idea, and actually practicing that truth with consistency and courage.

And that is ultimately what it comes down to. The first principle of non-violence is courage. Though my resolve has not yet been tested, I am fairly certain that if and when it is tested, my courage will fail and I will resort to the default human response, which is to meet violence with violence. Do I know that such a response is wrong? Yes. Do I know that violence will not solve anything, but will likely only make things worse? Yes. But until placed in a situation which forces me to choose between violence and non-violence, I do not know how I will respond. I fear I will not have the courage or creativity to non-violently resist someone who is attacking me, my wife, or my children. Yet such honesty is the first step in the journey toward non-violent resistance. Some of this will be discussed further in the section on "The Right to Bear Arms" in the following chapter.

Though United States Christians may have the legal right to bear arms under the protection of our Constitution, we do not have the gospel right. Jesus invites us to follow Him in dying for our enemies, rather than telling them to die for us.

JESUS PROVIDES THE RIGHT EXAMPLE

The greatest example of how to give up our rights is Jesus Christ.

Though as God incarnate, He had every right to life, liberty, and the pursuit of His own personal happiness, though He had the ultimate freedom to make His own religion, to say whatever He wanted to whomever, to call crowds of disciples to follow after Him, and to take up all the power and force of the universe in His defense, Jesus instead chose to give it all away.

Rather than fight for His right to life, He went freely to His death, even to death on a cross (Php 2:8). Though He had the freedom and liberty to do whatever He wanted, He came instead to proclaim liberty to the captives (Luke 4:18), and give freedom to a world enslaved in sin (John 8:36). In His life and teachings, He showed that true happiness is not in self-fulfillment, but in self-sacrifice and service (Matt 5:1-10; John 13:1-17). Jesus did not create a new religion, but set us free from all the rules and regulations of religion (The Gospels). When given the opportunity to slander others or speak in His own defense, He kept silent and spoke not a word (Matt 26:62; Mark 14:61). When crowds gathered to follow Him, He more often than not turned them away and kept His group of followers small (John 6:66). And far from taking up the sword and calling angels to defend Him against His enemies, Jesus told His followers to put away their sword (Matt 26:51), and did not call legions of angels for protection (Matt 26:53).

All of our God-given rights which we fight to defend and protect were discarded and rejected by Jesus. "When did Jesus ever concern Himself with protecting His rights or the rights of the community He was founding? Did He not rather do the exact opposite and teach us to do the same?"[23] He had more right to these rights than we ever will, but He gave them all up for the sake of His mission to inaugurate the Kingdom of Heaven on earth. If we are going to follow Jesus in helping His kingdom advance, we too must give up our rights and follow where He leads.

DISCUSSION QUESTIONS

1. What are the four "Rights" discussed in this chapter and where do they come from? Do you think that these rights are "biblical"?

2. Is the freedom of religion the same thing as the right to practice religion?

3. Even though we have the "Separation of Church and State" in the United States, who really grants churches the permission to exist? Who should we turn to when we need help defending our so-called rights? Who do we truly depend upon for our livelihood?

4. What are three different ways many people respond to government infringement?

5. By looking to the government to affirm our right to practice religion, what do we give up?

6. What are some ways the "church" has abused the freedom of speech?

---

[23] Boyd, *The Myth of a Christian Nation*, 181.

7. When we use our freedom of speech to speak things without love, are we actually serving God or ourselves? Why?

8. What are some things that can help us understand the words of Jesus in Matthew 23? Do these words from Jesus give us permission to blast our political opponents with harsh rhetoric? Why or why not?

9. How is Matthew 23 a litmus test for how we view God?

10. Who are the only group of people Jesus ever criticized? What does this tell us about who Christians can criticize?

11. How does a Christian truly practice the right to free speech?

12. What was the right to assembly really for? Does it have anything to do with religion and church?

13. What is the greatest myth of human history?

14. When we use war to fight for our freedoms, what are we taking away from others?

15. What is the only alternative to "Just War"?

16. What is Luke 22:36 really about? Is Jesus giving us permission to buy and use deadly weapons?

186 DYING TO RELIGION AND EMPIRE

17. Is fighting for your rights really "Christian" if it means taking those same rights from other people?

18. What did you think about the explanation of "non-violent resistance" in this chapter? Do you think it would "work" in real-world conflicts? Why or why not?

CONCLUSION

*If what you call your "faith" in Christ does not involve
taking the slightest notice of what he says, then it is not
faith at all—not faith or trust in Him, but only intel-
lectual acceptance of some theory of Him.*
—C. S. Lewis

The beautiful thing about following Jesus is that while He leads
us all in the same direction, there are millions of different paths
He can take to get us there. His goal, of course, is to advance the
Kingdom of God on earth through the people of God who are
being conformed into the image of God.

Throughout history, God has used the various forms of His
church and various approaches to government to bring about the
changes in this world He wants to see. Some forms of church and
government have been more effective than others, but no form of
either has ever been exactly what God wanted for all time. No
form of church or government in all of history has ever been
equivalent to what God intends His Kingdom to look like in this
world. Therefore, we must always be tuned in to the whispering
of the Holy Spirit as we seek to understand the will of God in our
day and time. Change is always occurring, and only those who

listen will catch the new wave of God in human history. Let me echo the words of Hans Küng from his groundbreaking and trouble-causing book *The Church:*

> It would be fatal for the Church to see itself primarily as a powerful factor in public life, as a high-powered combine, as a cultural and educational force, as the guardian of culture (Western culture, of course), as the bastion of "tradition" or the establishment, as a slightly more pious pressure group among many pressure groups, competing with others for power in politics, the arts, education, and economics. If it did this the Church would be abdicating as a Church, forgetting the crucial element which alone can make its visible aspects into a true Church: the Spirit, which invisibly controls the visible Church, making it spiritually alive, fruitful, and credible.[1]

I do not claim to have an infallible sense of what the Spirit is doing in the world and God's church today. I do sense, however, that change is rapidly taking place around us, and this book presents some suggestions for how we all can participate in these changes of God. These suggested changes are not theoretical only, but are ways I have been using to follow Jesus in my own daily living, and as I do, I have discovered more and more fellow travelers along the road.

You may find yourself traveling down a different road. That is fine. The goal is not to make sure that we are all on the same road, but that we are all following Jesus in the same direction. What has been proposed in the preceding chapters is simply a description of the road Jesus is leading me down.

[1] Hans Küng, *The Church* (Garden City, NY: Image Books, 1976), 62-63.

Ultimately, the question we must ask is not so much "What works?" in maintaining our national identity and way of life, but rather, "What looks most like Jesus?" and especially, Jesus dying on the cross. When we get the desire to hang on to our life the way it is, with our ease and comfort, with our rights and our liberties, we must call to ourselves in the same way Patrick Henry called to his fellow patriots to join his cause. We can say:

> Is life so dear, liberty so sweet, or happiness so important, as to be purchased at the price of putting others to death or taking away their liberties and freedoms so that we might protect our own? Forbid it, Almighty God! I do not know what course others may take, but as for me, I follow Jesus in saying "Give others liberty, even if it means my death!"

Death is not the end, and life is not so important that I would seek to hold off my death a few extra years by snuffing out the lives of others, or make my life a bit more sweet by causing others to live in hell. May we all, like Jesus, die to religion and empire by giving up what is religiously and legally "ours" so that through our death, others might have life. May we, like Jesus, make ourselves of no reputation, take the form of a bondservant, and humble ourselves for others, becoming obedient unto God, even to the point of death. Only in this way will God highly exalt Himself so that through our words, our actions, and our death, every knee should bow and every tongue confess that Jesus Christ is Lord.

ABOUT JEREMY MYERS

Jeremy Myers is an author, blogger, podcaster, and Bible teacher. Much of his content can be found at RedeemingGod.com, where he seeks to help liberate people from the shackles of religion. He lives in Oregon with his wife and three beautiful daughters.

If you appreciated the content of this book, would you consider recommending it to your friends and leaving a review on Amazon? Thanks!

JOIN JEREMY MYERS AND LEARN MORE

Take Bible and theology courses by joining Jeremy at
RedeemingGod.com/join/

Receive updates about free books, discounted books, and new books by joining Jeremy at
RedeemingGod.com/read-books/

SKELETON CHURCH: A BARE-BONES DEFINITION OF CHURCH (PREFACE TO "THE CLOSE YOUR CHURCH FOR GOOD" BOOK SERIES)

The church has a skeleton which is identical in all types of churches. Unity and peace can develop in Christianity if we recognize this skeleton as the simple, bare-bones definition of church. But when we focus on the outer trappings—the skin, hair, and eye color, the clothes, the muscle tone, and other outward appearances—division and strife form within the church.

Let us return to the skeleton church and grow in unity once again.

REVIEWS FROM AMAZON

My church gathering is struggling to break away from traditions which keep us from following Jesus into the world. Jeremy's book lends encouragement and helpful information to groups like us. –Robert A. White

I worried about buying another book that aimed at reducing things to a simple minimum, but the associations of the author along with the price gave me reason to hope and means to see. I really liked this book. First, because it wasn't identical to what other simple church people are saying. He adds unique elements that are worth reading. Second, the size is small enough to read, think, and pray about without getting lost. –Abel Barba

In *Skeleton Church*, Jeremy Myers makes us rethink church. For Myers, the church isn't a style of worship, a row of pews, or even a building. Instead, the church is the people of God, which provides the basic skeletal structure of the church. The muscles, parts, and flesh of the church are how we carry Jesus' mission into our own neighborhoods in our own unique ways. This eBook will make you see the church differently. –Travis Mamone

This book gets back to the basics of the New Testament church— who we are as Christians and what our perspective should be in the world we live in today. Jeremy cuts away all the institutional layers of a church and gets to the heart of our purpose as Christians in the world we live in and how to affect the people around us with God heart and view in mind. Not a physical church in mind. It was a great book and I have read it twice now. –Vaughn Bender

The Skeleton Church … Oh. My. Word. Why aren't more people reading this!? It was well-written, explained everything beautifully, and it was one of the best explanations of how God intended for church to be. Not to mention an easy read! The author took it all apart, the church, and showed us how it should be. He made it real. If you are searching to find something or someone to show you what God intended for the church, this is the book you need to read. –Ericka

Purchase the Paperback
Purchase the eBook

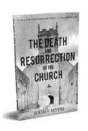

THE DEATH AND RESURRECTION OF THE CHURCH (VOLUME 1 IN THE "CLOSE YOUR CHURCH FOR GOOD" BOOK SERIES)

In a day when many are looking for ways to revitalize the church, Jeremy Myers argues that the church should die.

This is not only because of the universal principle that death precedes resurrection, but also because the church has adopted certain Satanic values and goals and the only way to break free from our enslavement to these values is to die.

But death will not be the end of the church, just as death was not the end of Jesus. If the church follows Jesus into death, and even to the hellish places on earth, it is only then that the church will rise again to new life and vibrancy in the Kingdom of God.

REVIEWS FROM AMAZON

I have often thought on the church and how its acceptance of corporate methods and assimilation of cultural media mores taints its mission but Jeremy Myers eloquently captures in words the true crux of the matter—that the church is not a social club for do-gooders but to disseminate the good news to all the nooks and crannies in the world and particularly and primarily those bastions in the reign of evil. That the "gates of Hell" Jesus pronounces indicate that the church is in an offensive, not defensive, posture as gates are defensive structures.

I must confess that in reading I was inclined to be in agreement as many of the same thinkers that Myers riffs upon have influenced me also—Walter Wink, Robert Farrar Capon, Greg Boyd, NT Wright, etc. So as I read, I frequently nodded my head in agreement. –GN Trifanaff

The book is well written, easy to understand, organized and consistent thoughts. It rightfully makes the reader at least think about things as … is "the way we have always done it" necessarily the Biblical or Christ-like way, or is it in fact very sinful?! I would recommend the book for pastors and church officers; those who have the most moving-and-shaking clout to implement changes, or keep things the same. –Joel M. Wilson

Absolutely phenomenal. Unless we let go of everything Adamic in our nature, we cannot embrace anything Christlike. For the church to die, we the individual temples must dig our graves. It is a must read for all who take issues about the body of Christ seriously. –Mordecai Petersburg

Purchase the eBook
Purchase the Paperback

PUT SERVICE BACK INTO THE CHURCH SERVICE (VOLUME 2 IN THE "CLOSE YOUR CHURCH FOR GOOD" BOOK SERIES)

Churches around the world are trying to revitalize their church services. There is almost nothing they will not try. Some embark on multi-million dollar building campaigns while others sell their buildings to plant home churches. Some hire celebrity pastors to attract crowds of people, while others hire no clergy so that there can be open sharing in the service.

Yet despite everything churches have tried, few focus much time, money, or energy on the one thing that churches are supposed to be doing: loving and serving others like Jesus.

Put Service Back into the Church Service challenges readers to follow a few simple principles and put a few ideas into practice which will help churches of all types and sizes make serving others the primary emphasis of a church service.

Reviews from Amazon

Jeremy challenges church addicts, those addicted to an unending parade of church buildings, church services, Bible studies, church programs and more to follow Jesus into our communities, communities filled with lonely, hurting people and BE the church, loving the people in our world with the love of Jesus. Do we need another training program, another seminar, another church building, a re-modeled church building, more staff, updated music, or does our world need us, the followers of Jesus, to BE the church in the world? The book is well-written, challenging and a book that really can make a difference not only in our churches, but also and especially in our neighborhoods and communities. –Charles Epworth

Do you ever have an unexplained frustration with your church, its service or programs? Do you ever feel like you are "spinning your wheels" when it comes to reaching others for Christ? This book helps to explain why this might be happening, and presents a convincing argument for why today's church services are mostly ineffective and inefficient. You will read concepts explained that you've not fully heard before. And you will get hints as to how it could, or should, work. –MikeM

Purchase the eBook
Purchase the Paperback

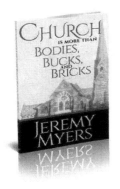

CHURCH IS MORE THAN BODIES, BUCKS, & BRICKS (VOLUME 4 IN THE "CLOSE YOUR CHURCH FOR GOOD" BOOK SERIES)

Many people define church as a place and time where people gather, a way for ministry money to be given and spent, and a building in which people regularly meet on Sunday mornings.

In this book, author and blogger Jeremy Myers shows that church is more than bodies, bucks, and bricks.

Church is the people of God who follow Jesus into the world, and we can be the church no matter how many people we are with, no matter the size of our church budget, and regardless of whether we have a church building or not.

By abandoning our emphasis on more people, bigger budgets, and newer buildings, we may actually liberate the church to better follow Jesus into the world.

REVIEWS FROM AMAZON

This book does more than just identify issues that have been bothering me about church as we know it, but it goes into history and explains how we got here. In this way it is similar to Viola's *Pagan Christianity*, but I found it a much more enjoyable read. Jeremy goes into more detail on the three issues he covers as well as giving a lot of practical advice on how to remedy these situations. –Portent

This book surprised me. I have never read anything from this author previously. The chapters on the evolution of the tithe were eye openers. This is something that has bothered me for years in the ministry. It may be truth that is too expensive to believe when it comes to feeding the monster. –Karl Ingersoll

Since I returned from Africa 20 years ago I have struggled with going to church back in the States. This book helped me not feel guilty and has helped me process this struggle. It is challenging and overflows with practical suggestions. He loves the church despite its imperfections and suggests ways to break the bondage we find ourselves in. –Truealian

Jeremy Meyers always writes a challenging book ... It seems the American church (as a whole) is very comfortable with the way things are ... The challenge is to get out of the brick and mortar buildings and stagnant programs and minister to the needy in person with funds in hand to meet their needs especially to the widows and orphans as we are directed in the scriptures. –GGTexas

Purchase the eBook
Purchase the Paperback

CRUCIFORM PASTORAL LEADERSHIP (VOLUME 5 IN THE "CLOSE YOUR CHURCH FOR GOOD" BOOK SERIES)

This book is forthcoming in early 2017.

The final volume in the *Close Your Church for Good* book series look at issues related to pastoral leadership in the church. It discusses topics such as preaching and pastoral pay from the perspective of the cross.

The best way pastors can lead their church is by following Jesus to the cross!

This book will be published in early 2020.

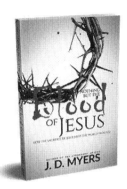

NOTHING BUT THE BLOOD OF JESUS: HOW THE SACRIFICE OF JESUS SAVES THE WORLD FROM SIN

Do you have difficulties reconciling God's behavior in the Old Testament with that of Jesus in the New?

Do you find yourself trying to rationalize God's violent demeanor in the Bible to unbelievers or even to yourself?

Does it seem disconcerting that God tells us not to kill others but He then takes part in some of the bloodiest wars and vindictive genocides in history?

The answer to all such questions is found in Jesus on the cross. By focusing your eyes on Jesus Christ and Him crucified, you come to understand that God was never angry at human sinners, and that no blood sacrifice was ever needed to purchase God's love, forgiveness, grace, and mercy.

In *Nothing but the Blood of Jesus*, J. D. Myers shows how the death of Jesus on the cross reveals the truth about the five concepts of sin, law, sacrifice, scapegoating, and bloodshed. After carefully defining each, this book shows how these definitions provide clarity on numerous biblical texts.

REVIEWS FROM AMAZON

Building on his previous book, 'The Atonement of God', the work of René Girard and a solid grounding in the Scriptures, Jeremy Myers shares fresh and challenging insights with us about sin, law, sacrifice, scapegoating and blood. This book reveals to us how truly precious the blood of Jesus is and the way of escaping the cycle of blame, rivalry, scapegoating, sacrifice and violence that has plagued humanity since the time of Cain and Abel. 'Nothing but the Blood of Jesus' is an important and timely literary contribution to a world desperately in need of the non-violent message of Jesus. –Wesley Rostoll

So grateful to able to read such a profound insight into the Bible, and the truths it reveals, in this new book by Jeremy Myers. When reading both this book and the Atonement of God, I couldn't help but feel like the two disciples that walked with Jesus after His resurrection, scripture says that their eyes were opened…they knew Him… and they said to one another, 'Did not our heart burn within us while He talked with us on the road, and while He opened the Scriptures to us?'

My heart was so filled with joy while reading this book. Jeremy you've reminded me once more that as you walk with Jesus and spend time in His presence, He talks to you and reveals Himself through the Scriptures. –Amazon Reader

Purchase the eBook
Purchase the Paperback

THE ATONEMENT OF GOD: BUILDING YOUR THEOLOGY ON A CRUCIVISION OF GOD

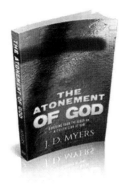

After reading this book, you will never read the Bible the same way again.

By reading this book, you will learn to see God in a whole new light. You will also learn to see yourself in a whole new light, and learn to live life in a whole new way.

The book begins with a short explanation of the various views of the atonement, including an explanation and defense of the "Non-Violent View" of the atonement. This view argues that God did not need or demand the death of Jesus in order to forgive sins. In fact, God has never been angry with us at all, but has always loved and always forgiven.

Following this explanation of the atonement, J. D. Myers takes you on a journey through 10 areas of theology which are radically changed and transformed by the Non-Violent view of the atonement. Read this book, and let your life and theology look more and more like Jesus Christ!

REVIEWS FROM AMAZON

Outstanding book! Thank you for helping me understand "Cru012
ision" and the "Non-Violent Atonement." Together, they help it all
make sense and fit so well into my personal thinking about God. I

am encouraged to be truly free to love and forgive, because God has always loved and forgiven without condition, because Christ exemplified this grace on the Cross, and because the Holy Spirit is in the midst of all life, continuing to show the way through people like you. –Samuel R. Mayer

If you have the same resolve as Paul, to know nothing but Jesus and Him crucified (2 Cor 2:2), then this book is for you. I read it the first time from start to finish on Father's Day ... no coincidence. This book revealed Father God's true character; not as an angry wrathful God, but as a kind loving merciful Father to us. Share in Jeremy's revelation concerning Jesus' crucifixion, and how this "vision" of the crucifixion (hence "crucivision") will make you fall in love with Jesus all over again, in a new and deeper way than you could imagine. Buy a copy for a friend—you won't want to give up your copy because you will want to read it again and again until the Holy Spirit makes Jeremy's revelation your revelation. –Amy

This book gives another view of the doctrines we have been taught all of our lives. And this actually makes more sense than what we have heard. I myself have had some of these thoughts but couldn't quite make the sense of it all by myself. J.D. Myers helped me answer some questions and settle some confusion for my doctrinal views. This is truly a refreshing read. Jesus really is the demonstration of who God is and God is much easier to understand than being so mean and vindictive in the Old Testament. The tension between the wrath of God and His justice and the love of God are eased when reading this understanding of the atonement. Read with an open mind and enjoy! –Clare Brownlee

Purchase the eBook
Purchase the Paperback

THE RE-JUSTIFICATION OF GOD: A STUDY OF ROMANS 9:10-24

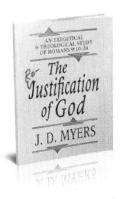

Romans 9 has been a theological battleground for centuries. Scholars from all perspectives have debated whether Paul is teaching corporate or individual election, whether or not God truly hates Esau, and how to understand the hardening of Pharaoh's heart. Both sides have accused the other of misrepresenting God.

In this book, J. D. Myers presents a mediating position. Gleaning from both Calvinistic and Arminian insights into Romans 9, J. D. Myers presents a beautiful portrait of God as described by the pen of the Apostle Paul.

Here is a way to read Romans 9 which allows God to remain sovereign and free, but also allows our theology to avoid the deterministic tendencies which have entrapped certain systems of the past.

Read this book and—maybe for the first time—learn to see God the way Paul saw Him.

REVIEWS FROM AMAZON

Fantastic read! Jeremy Myers has a gift for seeing things from outside of the box and making it easy to understand for the rest of us. The Re -Justification of God provides a fresh and insightful look into Romans 9:10-24 by interpreting it within the context of chapters 9-11 and then fitting it into the framework of Paul's entire epistle as well. Jeremy manages to provide a solid theological exegesis on a widely misunderstood portion of scripture without it sounding to academic. Most importantly, it provides us with a better view and understanding of who God is. If I had a list of ten books that I thought every Christian should read, this one would be on the list. –Wesley Rostoll

I feel the author has spiritual insight to scripture and helps to explain things. I would recommend any of his work! –Uriah Scott

I loved this book! It made me cry and fall in love with God all over again. Romans is one of my favorite books, but now my eyes have been opened to what Paul was really saying. I knew in my heart that God was the good guy, but J. D. Meyers provided the analysis to prove the text. I have been examining all the "proofs" about reformed theology because I was attracted to the message, but couldn't go all the way down the TULIP path, because it did not resonate in my heart that God who is Holy would love imperfectly. I believed Holy trumped Sovereignty, yet, I believe in the sin message, wrath of God, the Gospel and Jesus and decided that I was a "middle of the road" person caught between two big Theologies (the Big C and A). Now, I get it. I can with great confidence read the difficult chapters of Romans, and my furrowed brow is eased. Thank you, J. D. Meyers. I love God, even more and am so grateful that his is so longsuffering in his perfect love! Well done. –Treinhart

Purchase the eBook

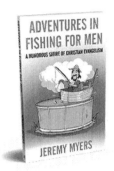

ADVENTURES IN FISHING FOR MEN

Adventures in Fishing for Men is a satirical look at evangelism and church growth strategies.

Using fictional accounts from his attempts to become a world-famous fisherman, Jeremy Myers shows how many of the evangelism and church growth strategies of today do little to actually reach the world for Jesus Christ.

Adventures in Fishing for Men pokes fun at some of the popular evangelistic techniques and strategies endorsed and practiced by many Christians in today's churches. The stories in this book show in humorous detail how little we understand the culture that surrounds us or how to properly reach people with the gospel of Jesus Christ. The story also shows how much time, energy, and money goes into evangelism preparation and training with the end result being that churches rarely accomplish any actual evangelism.

REVIEWS FROM AMAZON

I found *Adventures in Fishing For Men* quite funny! Jeremy Myers does a great job shining the light on some of the more common practices in Evangelism today. His allegory gently points to the foolishness that is found within a system that takes the preaching of the gospel and tries to reduce it to a simplified formula. A formula that takes what should be an organic, Spirit led experience and turns it into a gospel that is nutritionally benign.

If you have ever EE'd someone you may find Myers' book offensive, but if you have come to the place where you realize that Evangelism isn't a matter of a script and checklists, then you might benefit from this light-hearted peek at Evangelism today. –Jennifer L. Davis

Adventures in Fishing for Men is good book in understanding evangelism to be more than just being a set of methods or to do list to follow. –Ashok Daniel

Purchase the eBook

CHRISTMAS REDEMPTION: WHY CHRISTIANS SHOULD CELEBRATE A PAGAN HOLIDAY

Christmas Redemption looks at some of the symbolism and traditions of Christmas, including gifts, the Christmas tree, and even Santa Claus and shows how all of these can be celebrated and enjoyed by Christians as a true and accurate reflection of the gospel.

Though Christmas used to be a pagan holiday, it has been redeemed by Jesus.

If you have been told that Christmas is a pagan holiday and is based on the Roman festival of Saturnalia, or if you have been told that putting up a Christmas tree is idolatrous, or if you have been told that Santa Claus is Satanic and teaches children to be greedy, then you must read this book! In it, you will learn that all of these Christmas traditions have been redeemed by Jesus and are good and healthy ways of celebrating the truth of the gospel and the grace of Jesus Christ.

REVIEWS FROM AMAZON

Too many times we as Christians want to condemn nearly everything around us and in so doing become much like the Pharisees and religious leaders that Jesus encountered. I recommend this book to everyone who has concerns of how and why we celebrate Christmas. I recommend it to those who do not have any qualms in celebrating but may not know the history of Christmas. I recommend this book to everyone, no matter who or where you are, no matter your background or beliefs, no matter whether you are young or old. –David H.

Very informative book dealing with the roots of our modern Christmas traditions. The Biblical teaching on redemption is excellent! Highly recommended. –Tamara

Finally, an educated writing about Christmas traditions. I have every book Jeremy Myers has written. His writings are fresh and truthful. –Retlaw "Steadfast"

This is a wonderful book full of hope and joy. The book explains where Christmas traditions originated and how they have been changed and been adapted over the years. The hope that the grace that is hidden in the celebrations will turn more hearts to the Lord's call is very evident. Jeremy Myers has given us a lovely gift this Christmas. His insights will lift our hearts and remain with us a long time. –Janet Cardoza

I love how the author uses multiple sources to back up his opinions. He doesn't just use bible verses, he goes back into the history of the topics (pagan rituals, Santa, etc.) as well. Great book! –Jenna G.

Purchase the eBook

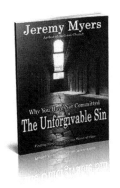

WHY YOU HAVE NOT COMMITTED THE UNFORGIVABLE SIN: FINDING FORGIVENESS FOR THE WORST OF SINS

Are you afraid that you have committed the unforgivable sin?

In this book, you will learn what this sin is and why you have not committed it. After surveying the various views about blasphemy against the Holy Spirit and examining Matthew 12:31-32, you will learn what the sin is and how it is committed.

As a result of reading this book, you will gain freedom from the fear of committing the worst of all sins, and learn how much God loves you!

REVIEWS FROM AMAZON

This book addressed things I have struggled and felt pandered to for years, and helped to bring wholeness to my heart again. –Natalie Fleming

A great read, on a controversial subject; biblical, historical and contextually treated to give the greatest understanding. May be the best on this subject (and there is very few) ever written. – Tony Vance

You must read this book. Forgiveness is necessary to see your blessings. So if you purchase this book, [you will have] no regrets. –Virtuous Woman

Jeremy Myers covers this most difficult topic thoroughly and with great compassion. –J. Holland

Good study. Very helpful. A must read. I like this study because it was an in depth study of the scripture. –Rose Knowles

Excellent read and helpful the reader offers hope for all who may be effected by this subject. He includes e-mails from people, [and] is very thorough. –Richie

Wonderful explication of the unpardonable sin. God loves you more than you know. May Jesus Christ be with you always. –Robert M Sawin III

Excellent book! Highly recommend for anyone who has anxiety and fear about having committed the unforgivable sin. –William Tom

As someone who is constantly worried that they have disappointed or offended God, this book was, quite literally, a "Godsend." I thought I had committed this sin as I swore against the Holy Spirit in my mind. It only started after reading the verse about it in the Bible. The swear words against Him came into my mind over and over and I couldn't seem to stop no matter how much I prayed. I was convinced I was going to hell and cried constantly. I was extremely worried and depressed. This book has allowed me to breathe again, to have hope again. Thank you, Jeremy. I will read and re-read. I believe this book was definitely God inspired. I only wish I had found it sooner. –Sue

Purchase the eBook
Purchase the Paperback

BOOK PUBLISHING INSTRUCTIONS: A STEP-BY-STEP GUIDE TO PUBLISHING YOUR BOOK AS A PAPERBACK AND EBOOK

The dirty little secret of the publishing industry is that authors don't really need publishing companies any longer. If you want to get published, you can!

This book gives you everything you need to take your unfinished manuscript and get it into print and into the hands of readers. It shows you how to format your manuscript for printing as a paperback and preparing the files for digital eReaders like the Kindle, iPad, and Nook.

This book provides tips and suggestions for editing and typesetting your book, inserting interior images, designing a book cover, and even marketing your book so that people will buy it and read it. Detailed descriptions of what to do are accompanied by screenshots for each step. Additional tools, tips, and websites are also provided which will help get your book published.

If you have a book idea, you need to read this book.

REVIEWS FROM AMAZON

I self-published my first book with the "assistance" of a publishing company. In the end I was extremely unhappy for various reasons

… Jeremy Myers' book … does not try to impress with all kinds of "learned quotations" but gets right to the thrust of things, plain and simple. For me this book will be a constant companion as I work on a considerable list of books on Christian doctrines. Whether you are a new aspiring author or one with a book or so behind you, save yourself much effort and frustration by investing in this book.
–Gerrie Malan

This book was incredibly helpful. I am in the process of writing my first book and the info in here has really helped me go into this process with a plan. I now realize how incredibly naive I was about what goes into publishing a book, yet instead of feeling over-whelmed, I now feel prepared for the task. Jeremy has laid out the steps to every aspect of publishing step by step as though they were recipes in a cook book. From writing with Styles and using the Style guide to incorporating images and page layouts, it is all there and will end up saving you hours of time in the editing phase.
–W. Rostoll

Purchase the eBook
Purchase the Paperback

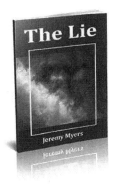

THE LIE – A SHORT STORY

When one billion people disappear from earth, what explanation does the president provide? Is he telling the truth, or exposing an age-old lie?

This fictional short story contains his televised speech.

Have you ever wondered what the antichrist will say when a billion people disappear from planet earth at the rapture? Here is a fictional account of what he might say.

Purchase the eBook for $0.99

JOIN JEREMY MYERS AND LEARN MORE

Take Bible and theology courses by joining Jeremy at
RedeemingGod.com/join/

Receive updates about free books, discounted books, and new books by joining Jeremy at
RedeemingGod.com/read-books/